SUPERSEDED

The Five Types
of
Legal Argument

The Five Types
of
Legal Argument

SECOND EDITION

Wilson Huhn

CAROLINA ACADEMIC PRESS
Durham, North Carolina

Library of Congress Cataloging-in-Publication Data

Huhn, Wilson Ray, 1950-
  The five types of legal argument / by Wilson Huhn. -- 2nd ed.
      p. cm.
  Includes bibliographical references and index.
  ISBN-13: 978-1-59460-516-1 (alk. paper)
  ISBN-10: 1-59460-516-5 (alk. paper)
  1. Law--United States--Methodology. 2. Judicial process--
United States. I. Title.

KF380.H84 2008
340'.11--dc22   2007044665

Carolina Academic Press
700 Kent Street
Durham, NC 27701
Telephone (919) 489-7486
Fax (919) 493-5668
www.cap-press.com

Printed in the United States of America

Contents

Preface

This book was written for students entering law school, so that from the first day they might appreciate what makes legal reasoning so fascinating and so difficult. I have presumed that the reader has a general knowledge of the American system of government and court system. I have used a sprinkling of specialized terms that are either defined in the text or that may be clarified by reference to a legal dictionary. It is my hope that this volume will also prove useful to attorneys and judges who may wish to consciously reflect upon the analytical skills that have become second nature to them.

This book is principally based on the article *Teaching Legal Analysis Using a Pluralistic Model of Law*, published at 36 Gonzaga Law Review 433 (2000/01) (copyright © 2001 Gonzaga Law Review Association). It also contains substantial material from *The Use and Limits of Syllogistic Reasoning in Briefing Cases*, 42 Santa Clara Law Review 101 (2002). The editors of the Gonzaga Law Review and the Santa Clara Law Review made important contributions that improved the clarity and the accuracy of this work.

I would like to thank my editor, Melissa Ulrich, Assistant Professor and Lead Faculty, Paralegal Studies, at The University of Akron for her many improvements to the text. I am also grateful to Judge Sam Bell and to several of my colleagues at The University of Akron School of Law, including Dean Richard L. Aynes, Associate Deans Elizabeth Reilly and Malina Coleman, and Professors Jane Moriarty, Samuel Oddi, Richard Cohen, Tracy Thomas, William Jordan, and Lloyd Anderson, for their valuable substantive and editorial suggestions. Finally, I would like to thank my research assistants, Matthew Hudson and Patrick Walsh, for their invaluable assistance. All errors and material omissions are, of course, my sole responsibility.

Above all, I am indebted to my wife and children for their love and support, and I dedicate this book to them.

Wilson Huhn

for
Nancy, Jesse, Niki, Missy, and David

Preface to the Second Edition

Among other changes, this edition of *The Five Types of Legal Argument* adds a new chapter, Chapter 23, setting forth a logical demonstration of the theory of the five types of legal arguments. This chapter demonstrates that the "brief" of a case takes the form of an argument of deductive logic, but that the different types of legal arguments are not the creatures of logic, but rather are the assumptions upon which all legal reasoning is based. This new chapter is based upon research originally published in the article *The Use and Limits of Syllogistic Reasoning in Briefing Cases*, 42 Santa Clara Law Review 813 (2002). I again wish to acknowledge the fine work of the editors and staff of the Santa Clara Law Review for their assistance in bringing that article to publication.

The most significant substantive change to the theory is contained in Chapter 10 of this edition where I have added two additional types of "intra-type" attacks on legal arguments. The first change is that I have identified another method of attacking intent arguments, and it is exemplified in two speeches by Abraham Lincoln. In addition, I have described another way of attacking tradition arguments that was employed by Justice Anthony Kennedy in the case of *Lawrence v. Texas*.

This edition updates references to *Regents v. Bakke* and *Bowers v. Hardwick* in light of the 2003 decisions of the Supreme Court in *Grutter v. Bollinger* and *Lawrence v. Texas*. In particular, the newer cases make contributions to our understanding of how to make and attack arguments based upon precedent and tradition.

I am grateful to the many law students, law professors, lawyers, and judges who have found this book to be useful in their pursuit of a deeper understanding of and facility with legal reasoning, as well as to those many persons who have made helpful suggestions for improving this book.

Wilson Huhn

The Five Types
of
Legal Argument

The Voices of the Law

The law is not smooth and pure like distilled water. It is instead a wild river, fed by tributaries which arise from myriad wellsprings. To master the law we must trace each and every legal argument to its source.

To use another image, the law speaks to us with different voices, and the greatest challenge we face in studying the law is to recognize and understand each of the voices of the law, and to express ourselves with every voice.

The most eloquent American jurist, Benjamin Nathan Cardozo, gave this description of "the nature of the judicial process:"

> What is it that I do when I decide a case? To what sources of information do I appeal for guidance? In what proportions do I permit them to contribute to the result? In what proportions ought they to contribute? If a precedent is applicable, when do I refuse to follow it? If no precedent is applicable, how do I reach the rule that will make a precedent for the future? If I am seeking logical consistency, the symmetry of the legal structure, how far shall I seek it? At what point shall the quest be halted by some discrepant custom, by some consideration of the social welfare, by my own or the common standards of justice and morals? Into that strange compound which is brewed daily in the cauldron of the courts, all these ingredients enter in varying proportions.[1]

---

1. BENJAMIN N. CARDOZO, THE NATURE OF THE JUDICIAL PROCESS 10 (1922). Cardozo, "a good and gentle soul," served on the United States

Cardozo accepted what we must struggle to understand. The law springs from multiple sources that often flow in different directions. As Professor Philip Bobbitt said, "[T]he values society labors to preserve are contradictory."[2]

Each of the five types of legal argument is like a single voice. In cases where they all lead to the same conclusion, the law is like a chorus singing the same tune. But where the different types of legal arguments lead to different conclusions—where they are in dissonance or cacophony—the analysis is difficult, and the proper interpretation of the law is unclear.[3] We must accept the fact that law

---

Supreme Court from 1932 to 1938. RICHARD A. POSNER, CARDOZO: A STUDY IN REPUTATION 3, 5, 9 (1990). While serving on the New York State Court of Appeals Cardozo authored a number of influential opinions which are still included in standard casebooks on torts and contracts. Lawrence A. Cunningham, *Cardozo and Posner: A Study in Contracts*, 36 WM. & MARY L. REV. 1379 (1995).

2. PHILIP BOBBITT, CONSTITUTIONAL INTERPRETATION 181 (1991). Bobbitt developed his influential theory of "modalities" to explain the interpretation of the United States Constitution. He describes these six interpretive modalities as "historical," "textual," "structural," "doctrinal," "ethical," and "prudential." *Id.* at x. William Eskridge and Philip Frickey developed an analogous model of statutory interpretation in which they suggest that in deciding what statutes mean courts take into account "textual," "historical," and "evolutive" considerations. William N. Eskridge, Jr. & Philip P. Frickey, *Statutory Interpretation as Practical Reasoning*, 42 STANFORD L. REV. 321, 322 (1990) (hereinafter *Practical Reasoning*). The five types of legal arguments that I describe in this book constitute, I believe, a more simple and more neutral "pluralistic" model of legal reasoning than those developed by Bobbitt, Eskridge, and Frickey. My model is also more comprehensive in that it applies to all areas of the law. The comparisons among these models of legal reasoning are set forth more fully in Wilson Huhn, *Teaching Legal Analysis Using a Pluralistic Model of Law*, 36 CARDOZO L. REV. 433, 453–457 (2001).

3. Akhil Amar uses a visual metaphor to illustrate the complementary function of the methods of interpretation: "[E]ach tool [of interpretation] is a lens through which to read, an imperfect but still useful lens whose reading must be checked against readings generated by other lenses." Akhil Amar, *Intratextualism*, 112 HARV. L. REV. 747, 801 (1999).

is often indeterminate.[4] Because law arises from several different sources, informed people of good will may legitimately differ as to what the law is in any particular case.

---

4. Professor Paul Wangerin has written how important it is for law students to develop tolerance for ambiguity: "[S]tudies suggest that as students move through law school, they rapidly develop an increased ability to see various sides of an issue and increased tolerance for ambiguity." Paul T. Wangerin, *Objective, Multiplistic, and Relative Truth in Developmental Psychology and Legal Education*, 62 TULANE L. REV. 1237, 1254–1255 (1988).

CHAPTER 1

The Purpose of Legal Education

Americans of the Revolutionary era and the early Nineteenth Century shared a profound faith in the concept of Natural Law, and fought to establish a government that recognized the "unalienable rights" of mankind. Alexander Hamilton said:

> [T]he sacred rights of mankind are not to be rummaged for among old parchments or musty records. They are written as with a sunbeam, in the whole volume of human nature, by the hand of Divinity itself and can never be erased or obscured by mortal power.[5]

Americans also believed that people in a pure and uncorrupted state were possessed of a natural sense of justice and an innate understanding of right and wrong. The archetype of the principled man of nature was Natty Bumppo, the hero of the Leatherstocking Tales by James Fenimore Cooper.[6] In Cooper's immensely popular nov-

---

5. Douglas W. Kmiec, *America's "Culture War"—The Sinister Denial of Virtue and the Decline of Natural Law*, 13 St. Louis U. Pub. L. Rev. 183, 188 (1993). The reliance of James Otis, Thomas Jefferson, and other Revolutionary leaders on this Lockean theory of natural rights is self-evident. Mark C. Niles, *Ninth Amendment Adjudication: An Alternative to Substantive Due Process Analysis of Personal Autonomy Rights*, 48 U.C.L.A. L. Rev. 85, 109 (2000).

6. The Leatherstocking Tales, in the order of the narrative, include The Deerslayer (1841), The Last of the Mohicans (1826), The Pathfinder (1840), The Pioneers (1823), and The Prairie (1827). The historian Perry Miller described the importance of these stories in shap-

els Bummpo confronted and resisted the march of American law and civilization.

Perhaps ironically, the leading legal scholars of the period concurred in this common belief that the laws of society are but a reflection (albeit imperfect) of the laws of nature. William Blackstone, for example, asserted that the law of nature "is binding over all the globe in all countries, and at all times; no human laws are of any validity, if contrary to this."[7] Leading American legal figures agreed, and contended that through the exercise of pure reason, rules of law are derived logically from fundamental first principles. For example, Nathaniel Chipman of Vermont confidently asserted that every law made under the Constitution "is ultimately derived from the laws of nature, and carries with it the force of moral obligation."[8] In a similar vein, Judge Peter Thatcher of Boston described legal analysis as "a patient deduction of truth from actual experiment and mathematical demonstration."[9] They considered the study of law to be a science like mathematics or the study of the laws of nature. The position expressed by Theodore Dwight at Columbia is typical: "[N]o science known among men is more strictly deductive than the science of a true Jurisprudence."[10]

---

ing American attitudes towards law in PERRY MILLER, THE LIFE OF THE MIND IN AMERICA 99–100 (1965) (hereinafter LIFE OF THE MIND).

7. *Id.* at 164. Legal historians who have traced the rise of legal formalism include Morton J. Horwitz, *The Rise of Legal Formalism*, 19 AM. J. LEG. HIST. 251, 255–6 (1975); John H. Langbein, *Chancellor Kent and the History of Legal Literature*, 93 COLUM. L. REV. 547, 568–569 (1993); and M. H. Hoeflich, *Law and Geometry: Legal Science From Leibnez to Langdell*, 30 AM. J. LEG. HIST. 95, 118 (1986).

8. MILLER, LIFE OF THE MIND, *supra* note 6, at 165.

9. *Id.* at 159.

10. *Id.* at 161. Professor Hoeflich credits Francis Bacon and Gottfried Leibniz with the identification of law with science and mathematics. Hoeflich, *supra* note 7, at 98–100. Dean Pound traced this thought to the "scholastic jurists" of the fourteenth and fifteenth centuries. ROSCOE POUND, INTRODUCTION TO THE PHILOSOPHY OF LAW 13, 15–16 (1965). Thomas Grey observed that "[t]he geometric ideal pervades the literature of the whole rationalist movement to create exact sciences of ethics, politics, and

Legal education reflected this belief that law is a science. In the early part of the 19th Century, the Law of Nations was an integral part of the curriculum at Litchfield, Columbia, and Harvard Law Schools because it was considered necessary to provide students with an adequate grounding in the general principles of law.[11] Lawbooks were doctrinal, setting forth the black letter law.[12] Professors lectured on the law, rather than engaging students in a dialogue, and students memorized rules, rather than studying cases.[13]

Into this setting strode Christopher Columbus Langdell, the greatest figure in American legal education. In 1869, the newly appointed Dean and Dane Professor of Law took his place at the front of the class for the first time at Harvard Law School, and called on a student: "Mr. Fox, will you state the facts in the case of *Payne v. Cave*."[14] Langdell revolutionized the methods of legal education, introducing the case method, Socratic discussion, and the casebook to the American law school.[15]

---

law that dominated European thought from Grotius to Kant, and that still remains strong in European legal scholarship today." Thomas C. Grey, *Langdell's Orthodoxy*, 45 U. Pitt. L. Rev. 1, 16 (1983).

11. *See* Scott T. Johnson, *The Influence of International Human Rights Law on State Courts and State Constitutions*, 90 Am. Soc'y Int'l L. Proc. 259, 273 (1996); Harold Hongju Koh, *The Globalization of Freedom*, 26 Yale J. Int'l L. 305, 312 (2001); and Roger S. Clark, *Steven Spielberg's Amistad and Other Things I Have Thought About in the Past Forty Years: International (Criminal) Law, Conflict of Laws, Insurance and Slavery*, 30 Rutgers L.J. 371, 435–436 (1998).

12. Marcia Speziale, *Langdell's Concept of Law as Science: The Beginning of Anti-Formalism in American Legal Theory*, 5 Vt. L. Rev. 1, 4–5 (1980).

13. *Id.*

14. Grey, *Langdell's Orthodoxy*, *supra* note 10, at 1.

15. "[H]e [Langdell] changed the method of law teaching from the study of general rules in textbooks or by lecture to the study of actual cases guided by the law professor's Socratic questioning." Thomas A. Woxland, *Why Can't Johnny Research? or It all Started with Christopher Columbus Langdell*, 81 Law Lib. J. 451, 455 (1989). "[P]rior to Langdell, and in the rest of the world, law was learned from the reading of treatises — *not* from the close and repetitive examination of countless appellate case opinions."

But despite all of these pedagogical innovations, Langdell clung to the notion that law is a science. He believed that legal principles led a life of their own, and that logic demanded adherence to them.[16]

Oliver Wendell Holmes, one of America's greatest jurists,[17] took issue with Langdell's concept of law as science, writing: "The life of the law has not been logic; it has been experience."[18] Thus began a revolution in the way that Americans think of law, in the way that lawyers and judges interpret the law, and in the way that students learn the law.

For the study of law is not a science. Rules of law are not immutable like laws of nature. Rules of law do not describe objective truth, they reflect subjective intentions. The lawyer's task is not to deduce the law from an unchanging set of first principles, but rather to predict how the law will emerge from a number of sources and a welter of conflicting values. As Holmes said, "The prophecies of what the courts will do in fact, and nothing more pretentious, are what I mean by the law."[19] Law students are not expected to mem-

---

Jeremy M. Miller, *The Science of Law: The Maturing of Jurisprudence into Fundamental Principles in Fairness*, 13 Western State L. Rev. 367, 388 (1986) (tracing the history of Natural Law and Positivism from ancient and medieval times up to the Hart/Dworkin debate of the 1970s and 1980s).

16. "Law, for Langdell, was emphatically a science, and the case method was the application of scientific inquiry to legal study. Inductive logic would be used to extract general legal principles from particular legal cases." Woxland, *supra* note 15, at 455.

17. At the outbreak of the Civil War Holmes enlisted in the Union army, assumed the rank of Captain, and was wounded in three battles. After the war, he earned an international reputation as a legal scholar. He served on the Supreme Judicial Court of Massachusetts for twenty years, and on the United States Supreme Court for thirty years. *See* Gary J. Aichele, Oliver Wendell Holmes, Jr.: Soldier, Scholar, Judge (1989).

18. Oliver Wendell Holmes, The Common Law 5 (Mark DeWolfe Howe, ed. 1963) (1881).

19. Oliver Wendell Holmes, *The Path of the Law*, 110 Harv. L. Rev. 991, 994 (1997), *reprinted from* 10 Harv. L. Rev. 457 (1897) (hereinafter *Path*).

orize all the rules of law, but are expected to learn how to persuasively argue for a favorable interpretation of the law or for a change in the law.

The curriculum in the first year of law school now consists of a number of courses thought to have practical importance, typically including Torts, Contracts, Property, Civil Procedure, Criminal Law, and Constitutional Law. In all of these courses students are expected to "brief" the cases, that is, to prepare a short summary of each judicial decision, setting forth the facts, the issue, the holding, and the court's reasoning.

Most students consider the "holding" of the court, which expresses the rule of the case, to be the most important part of the brief, and commit these case holdings to memory for use on examinations. Students do this because they believe that collectively these rules are "the law," and that studying law essentially consists of learning the holdings of the assigned cases and organizing them into a coherent pattern called the "outline" of the course.

It is true that in law school students dedicate thousands of hours to the job of memorizing the holdings of cases and preparing course outlines, and that this is no easy task. But memorizing case holdings and course outlines is only half of what students must learn in law school, and it is the easy half.

The truly hard part of law school, and the part that makes a legal education truly useful, is mastering the art of legal analysis. Students must learn not only the rules of law, the case holdings and course outlines, but must also learn how courts interpret the law and create it. It is not enough to know what the law has been; it is also necessary to develop the ability to predict what it may become. Students must master this skill because it is basic to representing clients competently.

The purpose of legal education is to teach students "how to think like lawyers." Students must learn how to make arguments for a favorable interpretation of an existing rule of law, or for the adoption of a new rule of law. To do this students must be able to recognize the different types of legal arguments, and understand the strengths and weaknesses of each type of argument. Thus, the purpose of legal education, and the purpose of this book, is to teach you how to identify, create, attack, and evaluate the five types of legal arguments.

CHAPTER 2

The Five Types of Legal Arguments

Legal arguments may be based upon *text, intent, precedent, tradition,* or *policy analysis.* Each type of legal argument springs from a different source of law. Each type of argument functions as a rule of recognition. Each type of argument is based upon a different set of evidence. And each type of argument serves different values.

1. The Five Types of Legal Argument Arise from Different Sources of Law

The five types of legal arguments represent different conceptions of what law is. Law may be considered to be legal text itself. It may be regarded as what the text meant to the people who enacted it into law. Law may be conceived of as the holdings or opinions of courts setting forth what the law is. It may be thought of as the traditional ways in which members of the community have conducted themselves. Finally, law may be understood as the expression of the underlying values and interests that the law is meant to serve. The five types of legal argument arise from these different sources of law.

2. The Five Types of Legal Argument Function as Rules of Recognition

The five types of legal arguments are a checklist of the kinds of legal arguments that may legitimately be made. This list is useful for law students who are preparing for class or writing a paper, lawyers who are drafting briefs or responding to questions in oral argument, and judges who are framing those questions or who are composing judicial opinions.

The types of legal arguments function like "rules of recognition." The legal philosopher H.L.A. Hart drew a distinction between primary rules of law—the rules governing behavior that we are obliged to obey—and secondary rules of law he called "rules of recognition." The rules of recognition are the rules that are used to create law. Hart said, "To say that a given rule is valid is to recognize it as passing all the tests provided by the rule of recognition and so as a rule of the system."[20] Perhaps the easiest example of a rule of recognition is that, to become law, a bill must be passed by a majority of both houses of Congress and must be signed by the President.[21] In an analogous way, the five types of legal argument tell us what is and what is not a valid legal argument. The five types of legal argument are the kinds of arguments that lawyers and judges accept as legitimate.[22]

3. The Five Types of Legal Argument Are Rules of Evidence for Determining What the Law Is

Whenever a question of fact is disputed at trial, attorneys call witnesses and offer exhibits to persuade the jury to decide the question in favor of their clients. In presenting this evidence, attorneys are bound by the rules of evidence. For example, to prove a fact at

---

20. H.L.A. HART, THE CONCEPT OF LAW 103 (1998).

21. U.S. CONST., Art. I, sec. 7, cl. 2. A bill may also become law if two-thirds of both houses of Congress vote to override a Presidential veto. *Id.*

22. Philip Bobbitt contends that the set of interpretive modalities he developed comprises the complete set of legitimate legal arguments interpreting the constitution. Philip Bobbitt, *Reflections Inspired by My Critics*, 72 Tex. L. Rev. 1869, 1913–1914, 1916 (1994) (hereinafter *Reflections*).

trial an attorney may not offer evidence that is hearsay or that is unfairly prejudicial.

In a similar fashion, whenever there is a question of law that is disputed at trial or on appeal, attorneys present evidence to persuade the court to decide the question of law in favor of their clients. But attorneys do not call witnesses to the stand or offer exhibits into evidence to prove what the law is. Instead they make and support legal arguments. Each type of legal argument is based upon a different set of evidence bearing on a question of law. The order in which I have listed the types of arguments suggests a progression in the scope of the evidence that is considered in determining what the law is.

Textual arguments place the strictest limitation on the evidence that is admissible to prove what the law is. Arguments based upon text consider only the constitution, statute, ordinance, or other legal document that is being interpreted. The interpretive method of "intent" expands the admissible evidence to include contemporary references indicating what was in the minds of the people who created the constitution, statute, ordinance or other writing. Examination of precedent is limited to statements of judges in formal legal opinions. Proof of tradition is more expansive, involving historical evidence of our people's beliefs and behavior patterns over decades or centuries. The scope of what may be considered by a court engaged in policy analysis is virtually unlimited. To support a policy argument a court may take judicial notice of any fact it finds relevant to determining the question of law.

4. The Five Types of Legal Argument Embody the Underlying Values of Our System of Laws

What are the general policies and values served by our system of law? What do we expect of the law? First, we expect the law to be clear and easily understood. It should be possible to present objective proof of what the law is. Second, we expect the law to reflect the choices made by the people who wrote the law. The law must respect the value of popular sovereignty (in the case of publicly enacted law) or of personal autonomy (in the case of contracts, deeds, and wills). Third, we expect the law to be consistent. The law serves as a guide to future action, so it must be stable and predictable. Fourth, we expect the law to conform to the settled expectations of society. The law should contribute to societal coherence. Fifth, we expect the law to be flexible enough to adapt to a changing society, so that it may reflect contemporary notions of justice.

Each type of legal argument serves a different value. Textual interpretation promotes objectivity. Legal arguments based upon intent reflect the popular will. Following precedent promotes stability. Following tradition promotes social cohesiveness. And policy arguments — consequentialist arguments — enable the law to adjust to changing conditions and to achieve justice.

These values are often in tension with each other. As we shall see in Chapters 16 to 22, some of the most difficult questions of law arise because different types of legal arguments give different answers to questions of what the law is. These differences often arise because people reasonably disagree as to which of the foregoing values — objectivity, popular sovereignty, consistency, coherence, or justice — should predominate in any particular case.

Each type of argument is described in more detail in the five chapters that follow.

CHAPTER 3

Text

The primary source of law in our society is legal text. Legal text includes the Constitution of the United States and the state constitutions, federal and state statutes, municipal ordinances, administrative regulations, and any other public writings that have the force of law. The term "legal text" also includes privately written documents such as contracts, wills, deeds, checks, and promissory notes. Although these private documents are not law in and of themselves, they are legal texts because they create or alter legal rights.

Historically, the commitment of law to writing has summoned obedience to the rule of law. In the ancient world, the Code of Hammurabi, the Decalogue of Moses, the Laws of Solon, and the Code of Justinian were crucial steps in the march of civilization. In the feudal period, written charters were prized for their ability to record and preserve the rights and obligations of the parties to feudal contracts.[23] In 1787 the founders of our nation committed our Constitution to writing so that it might be considered binding law, making possible the creation of a government under law.[24]

---

23. In the south of France, "the custom of using charters to preserve the record of vassalage was in common use from the beginning of the twelfth century onwards." F.L. GANSHOF, FEUDALISM 81 (1964).

24. "The powers of the legislature are defined and limited; and that those limits may not be mistaken, or forgotten, the constitution is written. To what purpose are powers limited, and to what purpose is that limitation committed to writing, if these limits may, at any time, be passed by those intended to be restrained?" Marbury v. Madison, 5 U.S. 137, 176 (1803) (Marshall, J.).

At the present time, in many areas of the law, law is not binding until it is reduced to writing. In many jurisdictions the criminal law is not effective until enacted in the form of written statute.[25] Substantive administrative regulations are not effective until published in the Federal Register.[26] Under the Statute of Frauds and the Parol Evidence Rule, certain kinds of contracts and contractual terms must be in written form,[27] and in general, to be effective, a will must be in writing.[28] In modern times, legal text forms the backbone of the law.

There are areas of the law that are not governed by controlling legal text. The law of tort, contract, and property, for example, are primarily based upon the "common law." The common law is the law that is expressed in judicial opinions. It is the law that has accumulated over centuries in hundreds of thousands of cases decided by the courts.

But the areas of common law are shrinking relative to text-bound law. As society becomes more complex, legislatures have enacted detailed statutes and comprehensive codes to bring uniformity and consistency to areas formerly governed by decisional law. For example, the Rules of Evidence, the Rules of Civil Procedure, and

---

25. *See* Wayne R. LaFave & Austin W. Scott, Jr., Substantive Criminal Law § 2.1, at 92 (1986). *See, e.g.,* Ohio Rev. Code Ann. § 2901.03(A), (Anderson 1999) which provides, "No conduct constitutes a criminal offense against the state unless it is defined as an offense in the Revised Code."

26. The Administrative Procedure Act states: "General notice of proposed rule making shall be published in the Federal Register...." 5 U.S.C. 553(b); and "The required publication...of a substantive rule shall be made not less than 30 days before its effective date...." 5 U.S.C. 553(d).

27. The Statute of Frauds requires written evidence of particular kinds of contracts, and the Parol Evidence Rule bars evidence that supplements or contradicts the terms of written contracts in certain circumstances. *See, e.g.* U.C.C. 2-201 and 2-202, for the statute of frauds and parol evidence rule governing the sale of goods.

28. *See, e.g.,* Unif. Probate Code 2-502.

the Uniform Commercial Code have all replaced the slow accretion of law under the case method in their respective areas.

In addition, our legislatures have created specialized administrative agencies that have the expertise to regulate intricate social problems. Every day these agencies collectively issue more law than an individual could learn in a year, governing every aspect of society, including the environment, the workplace, the commercial markets, taxation, and benefits programs.

However, the slow demise of the common law has not diminished the importance of judicial opinions. Legal text is frequently unclear as applied to particular factual situations. Thus the examination and interpretation of legal text by courts has assumed critical importance in our society.[29]

There are three methods of textual interpretation. Text may be interpreted according to its plain meaning, with the help of canons of construction, and by means of intratextual arguments.

1. Plain Meaning

The plain meaning rule is, of course, exactly what it sounds like: legal text is to be interpreted according to its plain meaning. When courts interpret legal text according to plain meaning, it is equiv-

---

29. One of the important consequences of this movement from case law to legal text is that text constrains the discretion of judges and courts to say what the law is.

> Statutory and constitutional law differs fundamentally from common law in that every statutory and constitutional text—the starting point for decision, and in that respect (but that respect only) corresponding to judicial opinions in common law decisionmaking—is in some important sense not to be revised by the judges.

Richard A. Posner, *Legal Formalism, Legal Realism, and the Interpretation of Statutes and the Constitution*, 37 Case Wes. L. Rev. 179, 187 (1987) (hereinafter *Legal Realism*).

alent to saying that the text is so clear that it does not require resort to any of the other methods of interpretation.[30]

Sometimes the plain meaning rule is stated with an important qualification. Many courts have observed that legal text should be given its plain meaning only if this would not lead to an absurd result.[31] For example, in *Green v. Bock Laundry Machine Co.*,[32] the United States Supreme Court rejected a "plain meaning" approach to interpreting Evidence Rule 609. The Court explained: "The Rule's plain language commands weighing of prejudice to a defendant in a civil trial as well as in a criminal trial. But that literal reading would compel an odd result in a case like this."[33] The Court in *Green* instead relied upon an extensive review of the legislative history of the Rule to determine its meaning.[34]

The leading contemporary advocate of "plain meaning" is Supreme Court Justice Antonin Scalia.[35] Justice Scalia describes

30. Judge Patricia Wald has argued that legal text is simply a superior and decisive method of determining legislative intent: "The Plain Meaning Rule basically articulates a hierarchy of sources from which to divine legislative intent. Text comes first, and if it is clearly dispositive, then the inquiry is at an end." Patricia M. Wald, *The Sizzling Sleeper: The Use of Legislative History in Construing Statutes in the 1988–1989 Term of the United States Supreme Court*, 39 Am. U. L. Rev. 277, 285 (1990). Cardozo also recognized the primacy of legal text: "Where does the judge find the law which he embodies in his judgment? There are times when the source is obvious. The rule that fits the case may be supplied by the constitution or by statute. If that is so, the judge looks no farther. The correspondence ascertained, his duty is to obey." Cardozo, The Nature of the Judicial Process, *supra* note 1, at 14 (1922).

31. See Kent Greenawalt, Statutory Interpretation: 20 Questions 57 (1999) (hereinafter 20 Questions).

32. 490 U.S. 504 (1989).

33. *Id.* at 509.

34. The *Green* case is an example of "cross-type conflict" between text and intent. This case is discussed in more detail in Chapter 19.

35. Justice Scalia is acknowledged as the leader of a school of jurisprudence which favors "an uncompromising application of statutory plain meaning," which William Eskridge calls "the new textualism." William N. Eskridge, Jr., *Norms, Empiricism, and Canons in Statutory Interpreta-*

himself as "[o]ne who finds *more* often... that the meaning of a statute is apparent from its text...."[36] A typical example of Justice Scalia's textual approach is his opinion in the Administrative Law case *M.C.I. Telecommunications Corp v. American Telephone and Telegraph Co.*,[37] in which he relied upon plain meaning to interpret the Federal Communications Act of 1934. The F.C.C. had excused M.C.I. from the expensive requirement of filing a tariff, and A.T. & T., its major competitor, challenged the decision of the F.C.C. The legal question was whether the Communications Act gave the F.C.C. the authority to waive this requirement, which is one of the principal obligations that the Communications Act imposes upon telephone companies. The Act authorizes the F.C.C. to "modify any requirement" of the law. A majority of the United States Supreme Court held that this provision of the Act did not give the F.C.C. the authority to utterly dispense with the filing requirement, because this would not be a "modification" of a requirement but rather a "basic and fundamental change" in a requirement. In the following passage from his majority opinion Justice Scalia identified the issue and resolved it by defining the plain meaning of the text of the Act:

> The dispute between the parties turns on the meaning of the phrase "modify any requirement." Petitioners argue that it gives the Commission authority to make even basic and fundamental changes in the scheme created by that section. We disagree. The word "modify"—like a number of other English words employing the root "mod" (deriving from the Latin word for "measure," such as "moderate," "modulate," "modest," and "modicum")—has a connotation of increment or limitation. Virtually every dictionary we are aware of says that "to

---

tion, 66 U. CHI. L. REV. 671 (1999) (hereinafter *Norms*); Eskridge, *The New Textualism*, 37 U.C.L.A. L. Rev. 621, 623 (1990).

36. Antonin Scalia, *Judicial Deference to Administrative Interpretation of Law*, 1989 DUKE L. J. 511, 521 (1989)(hereinafter *Judicial Deference*).

37. 512 U.S. 218 (1994).

modify" means to change moderately or in minor fashion.[38]

Justice Scalia then quoted definitions of the word "modify" from
four leading dictionaries,[39] and held that " 'Modify' in our view,
connotes moderate change."[40] Because the F.C.C. had not simply
"modified" a requirement of the Act, but rather had waived a fundamental requirement, the Supreme Court held that it had acted
outside its statutory authority.

The dissenting justices in M.C.I. used other interpretive techniques, particularly intratextual arguments and intent arguments,
in concluding that the F.C.C. acted within its statutory authority in
waiving the requirement.[41] Both *Green* and *M.C.I.* offer examples
of clashes between text and intent, a common kind of "cross-type"
conflict. Cross-type conflicts, which arise when different types of
legal arguments yield different interpretations of the law, are the
subject of Chapters 16 to 22.

2. Canons of Construction

The plain meaning rule relies upon the definitions of particular
words and phrases to interpret text. In contrast, the canons of construction are rules of inference that draw meaning from the structure or context of a written rule.

There are dozens of canons of construction. A relatively common canon was used by the United States Court of Appeals for the
7th Circuit to interpret a provision of the Uniform Commercial

---

38. *Id.* at 225.

39. Justice Scalia quoted definitions from the RANDOM HOUSE DIC-
TIONARY OF THE ENGLISH LANGUAGE (2nd ed. 1987), WEBSTER'S THIRD
NEW INTERNATIONAL DICTIONARY (1981), OXFORD ENGLISH DICTIONARY
(2d ed. 1989), and BLACK'S LAW DICTIONARY (6th ed. 1990). *Id.*

40. *Id.* at 227.

41. *Id.* at 235–245.

Code in *Merrill Lynch, Pierce, Fenner & Smith, Inc. v. Devon Bank.*[42]
The Court phrased the canon in the following terms: "It is not beyond belief that statutes contain meaningless provisions, but a court
should treat statutory words as dross only when there is no alternative."[43] The same canon was invoked by Justice John Marshall in
Marbury v. Madison[44] to interpret a provision of the United States
Constitution: "It cannot be presumed that any clause in the constitution is intended to be without effect...."[45] Canons of construction
can be used to interpret any legal text: constitutions, statutes, regulations, ordinances, contracts, or wills.

There are two types of canons of construction: textual canons and
substantive canons.[46] Textual canons, like the one from the previous paragraph, operate like rules of syntax in that they are used to
infer the meaning of a rule from its textual structure or context.
Another textual canon of construction is expressio unius est exclusio alterius ("to say the one is to exclude the other"). This common canon of construction is used to draw a negative implication
from a positive statement. Justice Marshall invoked this canon in
Marbury as well: "Affirmative words are often, in their operation,
negative of other objects than those affirmed...."[47] The same textual canon of construction was utilized by the Supreme Court in

---

42. 832 F.2d 1005 (7th Cir. 1987).
43. *Id.* at 1008.
44. 5 U.S. 137 (1803).
45. *Id.* at 174.
46. Professor Greenawalt discusses the difference between "textual"
and "substantive" canons in 20 QUESTIONS, *supra* note 31, at 202–211.
William Eskridge and Philip Frickey identify three kinds of canons of statutory construction: "linguistic presumptions about what language means,"
"presumptions about external sources," and "substantive" canons. Eskridge,
Norms, supra note 35, at 674.
47. From the fact that the text of Art. III, sec. 2, cl. 2 grants original
jurisdiction to the Supreme Court in "cases affecting ambassadors, other
public ministers and consuls, and those in which a state shall be a party,"
Marshall inferred that the Supreme Court does not have original jurisdiction over a case involving the Secretary of State. 5 U.S. 137, 174.

Chadha v. I.N.S.[48] The issue in that case was whether the Constitution authorizes Congress to reserve to itself a "one-house legislative veto" over the decisions of administrative agencies; in other words, is it constitutional for one house of Congress to reverse the decision of an administrative agency? In *Chadha*, Chief Justice Burger drew a negative inference from the fact that the Constitution expressly gives one house of Congress unilateral power to act in only four circumstances: (1) the House of Representatives may initiate impeachments; (2) the Senate may try impeachments; (3) the Senate may confirm or reject nominees to federal office; and (4) the Senate may ratify or reject a treaty.[49] The Court stated: "Clearly, when the Draftsmen sought to confer special powers on one House, independent of the other House, or of the President, they did so in explicit, unambiguous terms."[50] As a result, the Supreme Court held that the "one house legislative veto" was unconstitutional.

While textual canons like expressio unius are based upon the linguistic context of the provision, substantive canons are interpretive principles that are derived from the legal effect of a rule. For example, the substantive canon "remedial statutes are to be liberally construed" creates a presumption enlarging the scope of legislative reform,[51] while the substantive canon "criminal laws are to be strictly construed," called the "rule of lenity," protects us against vague criminal statutes.[52]

---

48. 462 U.S. 919 (1983).

49. *Id.* at 955–56.

50. *Id.*

51. Justice Antonin Scalia ridicules this canon as one of his "most hated legal canards" in *Assorted Canards of Contemporary Legal Analysis*, 40 Case W. Res. L. Rev. 581, 581–586 (1989/1990) (hereinafter *Canards*).

52. There is sometimes sharp disagreement over the wisdom of applying a substantive canon of construction. For example, there is division over whether the rule of lenity should apply to environmental crimes. Compare Joshua D. Yount, *The Rule of Lenity and Environmental Crime*, 1997 U. Chi. Legal F. 607 (favoring the application of the rule of lenity to the interpretation of environmental criminal statutes), with David E. Fil-

There are dozens of textual and substantive canons of construction, many of which conflict with each other. The topic of "competing canons" is discussed in Chapter 11.

3. Intratextual Arguments

Intratextual arguments use one portion of the legal text to interpret another portion. In effect, the entire legal document — the constitution, statute, regulation, ordinance, or contract — may be used as a codex or dictionary to interpret the meaning of specific provisions. Interest in this third type of textual argument has enjoyed a resurgence since a noted scholar, Professor Akhil Amar, coined the term in his influential article *Intratextualism*.[53]

Intratextual arguments follow one of two formats: they either compare the words used in one part of the text with the words used in another part, or they deduce the meaning of portions of the text from their position within the organization of the text. Perhaps the most famous examples of this interpretive method appear in *McCulloch v. Maryland*,[54] where Chief Justice John Marshall[55] utilized

---

ippi, *Unleashing the Rule of Lenity: Environmental Enforcers Beware*, 26 ENVTL. L. 923 (1996) (opposing the rule of lenity in this context).

53. Akhil Amar, *Intratextualism*, *supra* note 3, at 748 (1999).

54. 17 U.S. 316 (1819).

55. John Marshall led a distinguished career of public service before being elevated to the Supreme Court. He served under General George Washington at Valley Forge; he was elected to the Virginia House of Delegates and Council of State; he attended the Virginia ratifying convention where he argued in favor of the proposition that the proposed federal courts should exercise the power of judicial review; he was elected to Congress; he went to France as a representative of the United States in the "XYZ Affair;" and he served as Secretary of State under President John Adams. As Chief Justice, John Marshall led the Supreme Court from 1801 to 1835. During that time he authored a series of decisions that strengthened the powers of the government of the United States and that placed our government under the law of the Constitution. CHARLES F. HOBSON, THE GREAT CHIEF JUSTICE: JOHN MARSHALL AND THE RULE OF LAW 3–5, 8, 12, 47–71,

both types of intratextual arguments to interpret the Necessary and Proper Clause[56] in defining the scope of the implied powers of Congress.

The issue in *McCulloch* was whether Congress had authority under the Constitution to create a Bank of the United States. Article I, Section 8 of the Constitution contains seventeen clauses conferring specific powers on Congress—the enumerated powers. The enumerated powers include the power to tax and spend, the power to regulate commerce, and the power to maintain an army and navy, but they do not expressly state that Congress has the power to create a bank. However, the last clause of Section 8—Clause 18, the "Necessary and Proper Clause"—gives Congress the authority to take all actions which may be "necessary and proper" for carrying into execution the foregoing powers. The federal government contended that the Bank of the United States was a "necessary and proper" means of facilitating its enumerated powers, and that the law creating the Bank was therefore constitutional. To interpret the Necessary and Proper Clause and to determine the scope of Congress' implied powers, Justice Marshall framed two questions. Are the implied powers of Congress limited to those actions which are "absolutely necessary" for carrying out the express powers?[57] And is the Necessary

---

111–149 (1996). Supreme Court historian Bernard Schwartz noted: "The nationalism nurtured at Valley Forge was to flourish in the great decisions by which were hewn the high road of the nation's destiny." BERNARD SCHWARTZ, A HISTORY OF THE SUPREME COURT 58 (1993).

56. Art I, sec. 8, cl. 18.

57. Justice Marshall framed the issue as follows:

The argument on which most reliance is placed, is drawn from the peculiar language of this clause. Congress is not empowered by it to make all laws, which may have relation to the powers conferred on the government, but such only as may be "necessary and proper" for carrying them into execution. The word necessary is considered as controlling the whole sentence, and as limiting the right to pass laws for the execution of the granted powers, to such as are indispensable, and without which the power would be nugatory. That it excludes the choice of means, and leaves to Congress, in each case, that only which is most direct and sim-

and Proper Clause an expansion or a limitation of the power of Congress?[58]

To address the first question, Marshall noted that the framers used the term "necessary" to describe the implied powers of Congress in the Necessary and Proper Clause, but used the words "absolutely necessary" in Article I, Section 10 when limiting the power of the states to impose duties. The Necessary and Proper Clause states: "The Congress shall have power to make all laws which shall be necessary and proper for carrying into execution the foregoing powers." In contrast, Article I, Section 10, Clause 2 says: "No state shall, without the consent of the Congress, lay any imposts or duties on imports or exports, except what may be absolutely necessary for executing it's inspection laws." Marshall concluded that the term "necessary and proper" was intended to be more expansive than the term "absolutely necessary." Marshall stated:

> It is, we think, impossible to compare the sentence which prohibits a State from laying "imposts, or duties on imports or exports, except what may be absolutely necessary for executing its inspection laws," with that which authorizes Congress "to make all laws which shall be necessary and proper for carrying into execution" the powers of the general government, without feeling a conviction that the convention understood itself to change materially the meaning of the word "necessary," by prefixing the word "absolutely."[59]

Marshall addressed the second question—whether the Necessary

---

ple. Is it true, that this is the sense in which the word "necessary" is always used?
17 U.S. 316, 413.
58. Marshall noted: "The counsel for the State of Maryland have urged various arguments, to prove that this clause, though in terms a grant of power, is not so in effect...." *Id.*
59. *Id.* at 414–415.

and Proper Clause was a limitation or an expansion of the powers of Congress—by observing that "The clause is placed among the powers of Congress [Article I, Section 8], not among the limitations on those powers [Article I, Section 9]."[60] Consequently, he concluded that the Necessary and Proper Clause should be considered to expand the power of Congress, rather than to limit it, and he ruled that Congress did have the power to establish the Bank of the United States.

Intratextual arguments are also a powerful technique for interpreting statutes. For example, in *Dunnigan v. First Bank*,[61] a bank had mistakenly paid a check after its customer had stopped payment on the check. The Connecticut Supreme Court was asked to determine the scope of the bank's liability under Section 4-403 of the Uniform Commercial Code. In making this determination, the court compared the provisions of 4-403 governing stop payment orders with the provisions of Section 4-402 governing "wrongful dishonor" cases, where a bank mistakenly refuses to pay a check that it should have paid. Section 4-403 states: "The burden of establishing the fact and amount of loss resulting from the payment of an item contrary to a stop-payment order... is on the customer." In contrast, Section 4-402 says: "A payor bank is liable to its customer for damages proximately caused by the wrongful dishonor of an item." The contrast between the two provisions persuaded the Connecticut Supreme Court that the liability of a bank under 4-403 was more limited than its liability under 4-402, and therefore it found in favor of the bank. The court said: "This difference in the scope of the language used in Sec. 4-403(3), as compared to that used in Sec. 4-402, is consistent with the notion that Sec. 4-403(3) is intended to impose a limited, rather than broad, form of liability on banks."[62]

In summary, textual analysis looks to the language used in the legal document under review, whether it is a constitution, a statute,

60. *Id.* at 420.
61. 217 Conn. 205, 585 A.2d 659 (1991).
62. 217 Conn. 205, 212–213, 585 A.2d 659, 663.

a regulation, a contract, or a will. There are three different textual methods of interpretation: the plain meaning rule, the canons of construction, and intratextual arguments. The plain meaning rule seeks an unambiguous definition of the words of the written rule.[63] The canons of construction draw inferences about the meaning of a rule from its textual or legal context. Intratextual arguments look to the placement of a provision of law within the organization of a document, or to the use of similar or dissimilar terms in other portions of the document, to determine the meaning of the provision.

---

63. It is this quest for objectivity and "bright-line" rules that draws many jurists and scholars such as Justice Hugo Black and Justice Antonin Scalia to the plain meaning analysis. Justice Cardozo, in contrast, said that he had "become reconciled to the uncertainty, because I have grown to see it as inevitable." CARDOZO, THE NATURE OF THE JUDICIAL PROCESS, *supra* note 1, at 166.

CHAPTER 4

Intent

The second source of law is the intent of the people who wrote the text. This principle is applicable to every area of the law, but it is called by different names in each area.

1. The Intent Behind the Constitution, Statutes, Regulations, Contracts, and Wills

In constitutional law this type of interpretive argument is known as "the intent of the framers" or "original intent."[64] In *The Federalist No. 78*, Alexander Hamilton argued that the Constitution is superior to legislative acts because "the intention of the people" is superior to "the intention of their agents."[65] Similarly, in *Marbury v. Madison*,[66] John Marshall repeatedly invoked the intent of the framers to interpret the Constitution. At different points in his opinion, Justice Marshall stated:

---

64. The foremost "originalist" in the field of constitutional law is Robert Bork, who set forth his theory of original intent in the landmark article *Neutral Principles and Some First Amendment Problems*, 47 IND. L. J. 1 (1971) (hereinafter *Neutral Principles*).

65. "If there should happen to be an irreconcilable variance between [the constitution and a statute], that which has the superior obligation and validity ought, of course, to be preferred; or, in other words, the Constitution ought to be preferred to the statute, the intention of the people to the intention of their agents." ALEXANDER HAMILTON, JAMES MADISON, & JOHN JAY, THE FEDERALIST PAPERS 395 (1982).

66. 5 U.S. 137 (1803).

> If it had been intended to leave it in the discretion of
> the legislature to apportion the judicial power between
> the supreme and inferior courts according to the will
> of that body, it would certainly have been useless to
> have proceeded further.... [67]

> It cannot be presumed that any clause in the Constitu-
> tion is intended to be without effect.... [68]

> Certainly all those who have framed written constitu-
> tions contemplate them as forming the fundamental
> and paramount law of the nation.... [69]

> Could it be the intention of those who gave this power,
> to say that in using it the constitution should not be
> looked into? [70]

> [I]t is apparent that the framers of the constitution con-
> templated that instrument as a rule for the government
> of *courts,* as well as of the legislature. [71]

Justice Marshall explained why the intent of the framers should
control the actions of the legislature: "That the people have an original right to establish, for their future government, such principles
as, in their opinion, shall most conduce to their own happiness is
the basis on which the whole American fabric has been erected." [72]
    The right of the people to govern themselves, the exercise of
which Marshall referred to as the "original and supreme will," [73] was
recognized in the Declaration of Independence, where it is stated
that governments "deriv[e] their just powers from the consent of the

---

67. *Id.* at 174.
68. *Id.*
69. *Id.* at 177.
70. *Id.* at 179.
71. *Id.* at 179–180.
72. *Id.* at 176.
73. *Id.*

governed." The interpretive method of "intent" arises from the fundamental principle of popular sovereignty.

The same type of legal argument is invoked to interpret statutes, but in such cases the interpretive principle is called "legislative intent" or "the intent of the legislature." Traditionally, this has been considered to be the principal method of statutory interpretation. Courts typically acknowledge that they are bound by the intent of the legislature.[74] Courts also consider the intent of administrative agencies in determining the meaning of regulations issued by the agencies.[75] Similarly, in accordance with the principles of freedom of contract and personal autonomy, the law of contracts looks to the "intent of the parties,"[76] and the law of wills seeks to give effect to the "intent of the testator."[77]

---

74. "Traditional treatises on statutory interpretation generally acknowledge the primacy of legislative intent...." Eskridge and Frickey, *Practical Reasoning, supra* note 2, at 325. "For the interpretation of statutes, 'intent of the legislature' is the criterion that is most often recited." 2A SUTHERLAND STATUTORY CONSTRUCTION 22 (Norman J. Singer, ed. 1992).

75. Lars Noah, *Divining Regulatory Intent: The Place for a "Legislative History" of Agency Rules*, 51 HASTINGS L.J. 255 (2000).

76. "In interpreting the words of a contract, it is generally said that we seek for the meaning and intention of the parties; but inasmuch as two parties may have had different meanings and intentions, the court must determine to which one of them, if to either, is legal effect to be given." 3 ARTHUR LINTON CORBIN, CORBIN ON CONTRACTS 33 (1963)(hereinafter CORBIN). "In the construction or interpretation of contracts, the primary purpose and guideline, or the controlling factor, and indeed the very foundation of all the rules for such construction or interpretation, is the intention of the parties." 17A AM. JUR. 2d *Contracts* § 350, at 364 (1991). In Chapter 19 there is a description of the potential conflict between the text of a contract and the intent of the parties.

77. "In interpreting a will, it is the meaning and intention of the testator that is sought...." 3 CORBIN, *supra* note 76, at 32–33. "Recognition of the fundamental axiom that the ascertainment and effectuation of the intention of the testator is controlling in the construction of wills is found in countless decisions." 80 AM. JUR. 2d *Wills* § 1140, at 250 (1991). "Interpretation is not an effort to determine what a decedent *should* have said, or what the average person *would* have meant by the words used, although

2. Evidence of Intent

Evidence of intent may be drawn from the text of the law itself, from previous versions of the text, from its drafting history, from official comments, or from contemporary commentary.

a. Evidence of Intent in the Text Itself

The intent of the drafters of the law is often set forth in the legal text itself. The most prominent example of textual evidence of the intent of the drafters is the Preamble to the Constitution of the United States:

> We, the people of the United States, in order to form a more perfect union, establish justice, insure domestic tranquility, provide for the common defence, promote the general welfare, and secure the blessings of liberty to ourselves and our posterity, do ordain and establish this constitution for the United States of America.

Statutes also often include language setting forth the purpose of the law. For example, Section 1-102 of the Uniform Commercial Code provides:

> (1) This Act shall be liberally construed and applied to promote its underlying purposes and policies.
> Underlying purposes and policies of this Act are (a) to simplify, clarify and modernize the law governing commercial transactions; (b) to permit the continued expansion of commercial practices through custom, usage, and agreement of the parties; (c) to make uniform the law among the various jurisdictions.

---

courts often do just this, notwithstanding protestations otherwise. Rather, the effort is to determine what this decedent meant by the words used." JEF-FREY N. PENNELL & ALAN NEWMAN, WILLS, TRUSTS, AND ESTATES 172 (2000).

Obviously, courts must give great weight to statements of purpose contained in the law under consideration.

b. Previous Versions of the Text

When the current version of a law differs from previous versions, the courts naturally infer that the drafters of the current law intended to change the law. This type of argument can be used to interpret a constitution or a statute.

As noted in Chapter 3, the question decided by the Supreme Court in *McCulloch v. Maryland*[78] concerned the constitutionality of the law creating the Bank of the United States. The issue that was discussed in that Chapter was whether the Necessary and Proper Clause gave Congress the power to establish the Bank. There was another issue decided in that case that also bore upon the question of the constitutionality of the Bank: did the creation of the Bank by Congress invade the reserved powers of the States? To resolve this question Justice Marshall compared the Constitution of the United States to the document that it replaced, the Articles of Confederation.

Article II of the Articles of Confederation provided: "[E]ach state retains its sovereignty, freedom, and independence, and every Power, Jurisdiction, and right, which is not by this confederation *expressly* delegated to the United States, in Congress assembled." (Emphasis added.) In contrast, the Tenth Amendment to the Constitution states: "The powers not delegated to the United States by the Constitution, nor prohibited by it to the States, are reserved to the States respectively, or to the people." The Supreme Court concluded that the omission of the word "expressly" in the Tenth Amendment of the United States Constitution was evidence that the framers intended to broaden the federal power and narrow the reserved powers of the States. Marshall said, "The men who drew and adopted this amendment had experienced the embarrassments resulting from the in-

---

78. 17 U.S. 316 (1819).

sertion of this word ["expressly"] in the articles of confederation, and probably omitted it to avoid those embarrassments."[79]

The same type of legal argument was used in *Diaz v. Manufacturers Hanover Trust Co.*,[80] a New York State case interpreting a provision of Uniform Commercial Code. The plaintiff, Diaz, had lost two certified checks that were payable to her and drawn on Manufacturers Hanover. The checks had not been cashed, so she sued to make the bank pay her the amount of the checks. The bank refused to pay the checks because if someone later turned up in possession of the checks and demanded payment, the bank would be liable again to the holder of the checks. The relevant provision of the New York State version of the Uniform Commercial Code required the plaintiff to post a huge indemnity bond before recovering on the checks. This requirement, in effect, prevented her from suing the bank. Did the court have the discretion to waive the requirement of the bond in the interests of justice? To determine the intent of the legislature the court compared the language of the standard version of the Uniform Commercial Code with the version that had been enacted by the State of New York. The standard version of the law provided: "The court *may* require security indemnifying the defendant...." In contrast, the version adopted by the New York legislature provided: "The court *shall* require security, in an amount fixed by the court not less than twice the amount allegedly unpaid on the instrument...." The court concluded that this change from "may" to "shall" was evidence that the legislature intended to require the posting of the bond:

> [T]he New York version of section 3-804 of the Uniform Commercial Code pointedly changed the word "may" to "shall," and the Legislature in 1964 further amended this section to fix the amount of security to be not less than twice the amount allegedly unpaid on the

---

79. *Id.* at 406–407.
80. 92 Misc. 2d 802, 401 N.Y.S.2d 952 (N.Y. Sup. Ct. 1977).

instrument.... Thus, our legislature appears to have considered the matter and amended the statute to make the furnishing of security...mandatory....[81]

This kind of argument that draws inferences about the meaning of legal text by comparing it to the language of other legal documents is called an "intertextual argument," as distinguished from "intratextual arguments" that draw inferences from language in the same legal text.[82]

c. The History of the Text

In *Village of Arlington Heights v. Metropolitan Housing Development Corp.*,[83] the Supreme Court generally identified five sources of evidence that could be used to ascertain the intent behind a governmental decision:

(1) The historical background of the decision;

(2) The specific sequence of events leading up to the challenged decision;

(3) Departures from the normal procedural sequence;

(4) The legislative or administrative history..., especially where there are contemporary statements by members of the decisionmaking body, minutes of its meetings, or reports; and

(5) In some extraordinary instances the members might be called to the stand at trial to testify concerning the purpose of the official action....[84]

The most common evidence of legislative intent is number (4),

---

81. 92 Misc.2d 802, 804, 401 N.Y.S.2d 952, 954.
82. Amar, *Intratextualism, supra* note 3, at 800.
83. 429 U.S. 252 (1977).
84. *Id.* at 267–268.

legislative history. As a bill becomes a law, each step in the legislative process is documented. These documents, known collectively as the "legislative history," include transcripts of legislative committee hearings, committee reports, and statements on the floor of the legislature. Some categories of legislative history are considered to be more authoritative evidence of legislative intent than others. Judge Abner Mikva and Professor Eric Lane rank the categories of legislative history in the following "rough pecking order," in terms of their importance for proving legislative intent:

> (1) Committee reports (including conference reports),
>
> (2) Markup transcripts [transcripts of meetings where a bill is read and discussed],
>
> (3) Committee debate and hearing transcripts,
>
> (4) Transcripts of "hot" (actual) floor debate.[85]

This subject, the hierarchy of categories of legislative intent, is discussed again in Chapter 12, Intra-type Attacks on Intent Arguments.

d. Official Comments

During the last half of the 20th Century a number of comprehensive codes were drafted to govern entire fields of law. These codes were intended to apply throughout the United States, either as federal law or as models for the enactment of uniform legislation by the States. Each of these codes has been accompanied by extensive official commentary in order to ensure uniform interpretation of the law. This influential category of proof of legislative intent includes the Official Comments to the Uniform Commercial Code, the Advisory Committee Notes accompanying the Federal Rules of Evidence, and the Advisory Committee Notes to the Federal Rules

---

85. ABNER J. MIKVA & AND ERIC LANE, AN INTRODUCTION TO STATUTORY INTERPRETATION AND THE LEGISLATIVE PROCESS 36 (1997).

of Evidence. These comments are extremely persuasive evidence of legislative intent.[86]

e. Contemporary Commentary

Commentary on the meaning of legal text around the time of its adoption is another important category of evidence bearing on the intent of the people who adopted the text into law. Law review articles are a common source of commentary on pending or newly adopted legislation, and are a secondary source of proof of intent.

In the field of constitutional law, one of the principal sources of "original intent" is the Federalist Papers,[87] a series of essays published by James Madison, Alexander Hamilton, and John Jay to promote the ratification of the United States Constitution. In *Printz v. United States*,[88] the justices of the Supreme Court referred extensively to the Federalist Papers. The majority opinion alone cited eleven *different* works of the Federalists.[89]

In summary, the intent of a law may be proven by a variety of methods. The text of a law, previous versions of it, its drafting history, official comments, and contemporary commentary all may contribute to our understanding of the intent of the framers of the text.

---

86. On rare occasions there are conflicts or perceived conflicts between the text of the law and the official commentary. This represents conflict between text and intent, which is discussed in more detail in Chapter 19.

87. *See supra* note 65. For a discussion of the use of the Federalist Papers as evidence of original intent *see* John F. Manning, *Textualism and the Role of The Federalist in Constitutional Adjudication*, 66 Geo. Wash. L. Rev. 1337 (1998).

88. 521 U.S. 898 (1997).

89. *Id.* at 910, 914, 918, 919, 921, and 922 (Scalia, J.).

CHAPTER 5

Precedent

Most of the law that people study in law school, and practically all of the law that is taught in the first year, is case law. From the first day of law school students are expected to brief cases and to discuss judicial opinions. In Constitutional Law, the first case that is assigned is usually *Marbury v. Madison*,[90] in which Chief Justice John Marshall said: "It is emphatically the province and duty of the judicial department to say what the law is."[91]

As Justice Marshall recognized, the courts are not mere agents of the legislative and the executive branches. Since the time of Sir Edward Coke and Sir Matthew Hale, distinguished judges who each served as Lord Chief Justice of England in the 16th Century, judicial precedent has been considered to be an independent source of law.[92] Common law legal systems such as that of the United States and Great Britain give great weight to prior judicial pronouncements on the meaning of the law, which are in many cases binding upon other courts addressing the same or similar issues. In

---

90. 5 U.S. 137 (1803).

91. *Id.* at 177. Justice Marshall made this assertion in support of the principle of judicial review, which is the power of the courts to declare acts of the legislature unconstitutional. In doing so Marshall was paraphrasing Alexander Hamilton, as he often did. In The Federalist No. 78, Hamilton had written: "The interpretation of the laws is the proper and peculiar province of the courts." *See* THE FEDERALIST PAPERS, *supra* note 65, at 395.

92. Harold J. Berman and Charles J. Reid, Jr., *The Transformation of English Legal Science: From Hale to Blackstone*, 45 EMORY L. J. 437, 446–449 (1996).

contrast, the civil law systems typical of the nations of continental Europe consider judicial decisions to be not a primary source of law, but merely advisory opinions about the meaning of a law.[93]

The principle of *stare decisis* (which literally means "to stand by things decided"[94]) is what lends strength to precedent. Stare decisis encourages courts to follow their own prior decisions, and it requires lower courts to follow decisions of higher courts in the same jurisdiction. The principle of stare decisis, however, applies only to the holding of the previous case. Judicial reasoning that is unnecessary to a decision (called *obiter dictum*) has no binding effect on later courts.

Perhaps the most dramatic invocation of stare decisis occurred in the case of *Planned Parenthood of Southeastern Pennsylvania v. Casey*,[95] in which the Supreme Court unexpectedly reaffirmed *Roe v. Wade*.[96] In their joint plurality opinion, Justices O'Conner, Kennedy, and Souter voted to follow *Roe* despite their doubts that *Roe* had been correctly decided.[97] After declaring that "Liberty finds no refuge in a jurisprudence of doubt,"[98] they articulated guidelines for reducing doubt by describing when constitutional precedent must be followed and when it may be overruled.[99] Those guidelines are examined in Chapter 13, "Intra-type Attacks on Precedent Arguments."

The use of precedent is essentially reasoning by analogy. The leading American authority on analogical reasoning was Edward Levi, who served as Attorney General of the United States and as

---

93. Nicolas Marie Kublicki, *An Overview of the French Legal System from an American Perspective*, 12 B. U. Int'l L. J. 57, 58 (1994).

94. Black's Law Dictionary (7th ed. 1999).

95. 505 U.S. 833 (1992).

96. 410 U.S. 113 (1973).

97. "[T]he reservations any of us may have in reaffirming the central holding of *Roe* are outweighed by the explication of individual liberty we have given combined with the force of stare decisis." 505 U.S. 833, 853.

98. *Id.* at 844.

99. *Id.* at 854–855.

Dean of the Chicago Law School. In the following much-cited passage from his book *An Introduction to Legal Reasoning*,[100] Levi described the process of analogical reasoning:

> The basic pattern of legal reasoning is reasoning by example. It is reasoning from case to case. It is a three-step process described by the doctrine of precedent in which a proposition descriptive of the first case is made into a rule of law and then applied to a next similar situation. The steps are these: similarity is seen between cases; next the rule of law inherent in the first case is announced; then the rule of law is made applicable to the second case.[101]

The first step — identifying a similarity between cases — is often difficult. What is it that makes one case similar to, or different from, another? Which points of similarity and dissimilarity are important?[102] The similarity of one case to another may be measured on two levels: facts and values. One may say that one case is similar to another because they are factually similar, or that one case is similar to another because they implicate the same underlying values. Whether a cited case is distinguishable from the case under consideration is another topic that is considered in Chapter 13.

---

100. Professor Larry Alexander refers to this as a "classic" work on legal reasoning. Larry Alexander, *The Banality of Legal Reasoning*, 73 Notre Dame L. Rev. 517, 523 (1998).

101. Edward Levi, An Introduction to Legal Reasoning 1–2 (1948).

102. This inquiry, which Steven Burton refers to as "the problem of importance," is discussed in Chapter 13.

CHAPTER 6

Tradition

The traditions of our people are the fourth source of legal authority. The common law was originally understood to be the customary law, the "law of the land." The common law did not purport to incorporate the wisest or most enlightened social policies. Instead, it reflected the customs of the people and the traditions of the community.[103]

The Supreme Court has identified "tradition" as a principal test for determining our fundamental rights. In *Palko v. Connecticut*,[104] Justice Benjamin Cardozo described our constitutional rights as those which are "so rooted in the tradition and conscience of our people as to be ranked as fundamental."[105] Justice Lewis Powell articulated a similar principle in *Moore v. City of East Cleveland*,[106] in which he said that our fundamental rights are those which are "deeply rooted in this Nation's history and tradition."[107] In *Bowers v. Hardwick*[108] Chief Justice Warren Burger invoked tradition in re-

---

103. Professor Cass Sunstein has written: "The common law ... has often been understood as a result of social custom rather than an imposition of judicial will. According to this view, the common law implements the customs of the people; it does not impose the judgment of any sovereign body." Cass. R. Sunstein, *On Analogical Reasoning*, 106 Harv. L. Rev. 741, 754 (1993).
104. 302 U.S. 319 (1937).
105. *Id.* at 325.
106. 431 U.S. 494 (1977).
107. *Id.* at 503.
108. 478 U.S. 186 (1986), *overruled* Lawrence v. Texas, 539 U.S. 558 (2003).

jecting a gay rights claim: "To hold that the act of homosexual sodomy is somehow protected as a fundamental right would be to cast aside millennia of moral teaching."[109] And in *Washington v. Glucksberg*,[110] Chief Justice William Rehnquist refused to recognize a constitutional right to assisted suicide on similar grounds: "[T]he question before the Court is ... properly characterized as whether the 'liberty' specially protected by the Clause includes a right to commit suicide which itself includes a right to assistance in doing so. This asserted right has no place in our Nation's traditions, given the country's consistent, almost universal, and continuing rejection of the right, even for terminally ill, mentally competent adults."[111]

Oliver Wendell Holmes cited tradition as a controlling factor on the constitutional question of federalism (the legal relation between the state and federal governments). In *Missouri v. Holland*[112] the issue was whether a treaty protecting migratory birds invaded the reserved powers of the states referred to in the Tenth Amendment.[113] In the following passage of his opinion Justice Holmes interpreted the Constitution in light of the nation's experience, rather than by reference to text or intent:

> [W]hen we are dealing with words that also are a con-
> stituent act, like the Constitution of the United States,
> we must realize that they have called into life a being
> the development of which could not have been fore-
> seen completely by the most gifted of its begetters. It
> was enough for them to realize or to hope that they had
> created an organism; it has taken a century and has cost

---

109. *Id.* at 197 (Burger, C.J. concurring).
110. 521 U.S. 702 (1997).
111. *Id.* at 703.
112. 252 U.S. 416 (1920).
113. The Tenth Amendment states: "The powers not delegated to the government of the United States, nor prohibited to the states, are reserved to the States and to the people thereof."

their successors much sweat and blood to prove that
they created a nation. The case before us must be considered in the light of our whole experience and not
merely in that of what was said a hundred years ago....
We must consider what this country has become in deciding what [the Tenth Amendment] has reserved.[114]

Similarly, Justice Felix Frankfurter identified tradition as an important element for measuring the scope of the President's implied
powers under the constitution. In *Youngstown Sheet & Tube v.
Sawyer*,[115] he stated:

Deeply embedded traditional ways of conducting government cannot supplant the Constitution or legislation, but they give meaning to the words of a text or
supply them. It is an inadmissibly narrow conception of
American constitutional law to confine it to the words
of the constitution and to disregard the gloss which life
has written upon them.[116]

Tradition is a powerful source of law in other areas as well. The
law of real property, in particular, has been molded by tradition.[117]
Likewise, the law of commercial transactions reflects custom and
tradition. The Uniform Commercial Code (U.C.C.), a comprehensive statute governing commercial transactions that has been
enacted in all fifty states, was deliberately drafted to conform to

---

114. *Id.* at 433–434.
115. 343 U.S. 579 (1952).
116. *Id.* at 610 (Frankfurter, J., concurring).
117. As Justice Cardozo observed: "Let me speak first of those fields
where there can be no progress without history. I think the law of real
property supplies the readiest example. No lawgiver meditating a code of
laws conceived the system of feudal tenures. History built up the system
and the law that went with it." CARDOZO, THE NATURE OF THE JUDICIAL
PROCESS,*supra* note 1, at 54.

traditional business practices.[118] The U.C.C. specifies that one of its primary purposes is "to permit the continued expansion of commercial practices through custom, usage and agreement of the parties."[119] The U.C.C. calls a traditional way of doing business a "trade usage,"[120] and under the U.C.C, trade usages supplement the meaning of contracts.[121]

An example of a legal argument based upon tradition appears in an opinion from the Virginia case of *Taylor v. Roeder*,[122] where the dissenting judge argued that promissory notes with variable interests rates are "negotiable instruments" within the meaning of the U.C.C.:

> Instruments providing that loan interest may be adjusted over the life of the loan routinely pass with increasing frequency in this state and many others as negotiable instruments. This court should recognize this custom and usage, as the commercial market has, and hold these instruments to be negotiable.[123]

Similarly, social traditions play an important role in the allocation of liability for tort. For example, courts have been reluctant to

118. "[W]hen Professor Llewellyn directed the drafting of the Uniform Commercial Code, he identified the best commercial practices of the day and wrote them into the Code." Robert Cooter, *Normative Failure Theory of Law*, 82 CORNELL L. REV. 947, 948 (1997).

119. U.C.C. 1-102(2)(b).

120. U.C.C. 1-205(2) provides: "A usage of trade is any practice or method having such regularity of observance in a place, vocation or trade as to justify an expectation that it will be observed with respect to the transaction in question."

121. U.C.C. 1-205(3) states: "A course of dealing between parties and any usage of trade in the vocation or trade in which they are engaged or of which they are or should be aware give particular meaning to and supplement or qualify terms of an agreement."

122. 234 Va. 99, 360 S.E.2d 191 (1987).

123. 234 Va. 99, 107, 360 S.E.2d 191, 196 (Compton, J., dissenting).

impose liability for serving alcohol to adults in social settings. In *Brandjord v. Hopper*,[124] a Pennsylvania court determined that there would be no liability for defendants who "engaged in the tradition of 'tailgating,' enjoying food and consuming several 12 ounce cans of beer which they had purchased together."[125] But courts that have dealt with this subject are not invariably wedded to tradition. In *Kelley v. Gwinnell*,[126] the Supreme Court of New Jersey proved unsympathetic to the custom of social drinking:

> Does our society morally approve of the decision to continue to allow the charm of unrestrained social drinking when the cost is the lives of others, sometimes of the guests themselves? If we but step back and observe ourselves objectively, we will see a phenomenon not of merriment but of cruelty, causing misery to innocent people, tolerated for years despite our knowledge that without fail, out of our extraordinarily high number of deaths caused by automobiles, nearly half have regularly been attributable to drunken driving. Should we be so concerned about disturbing the customs of those who knowingly supply that which causes the offense, so worried about their costs, so worried about their inconvenience, as if they were the victims rather than the cause of the carnage?[127]

Tradition often exerts a silent influence on legal reasoning. Our traditions establish "baselines," which are background assumptions that favor the status quo and place the burden of proof on any person who seeks to change the existing order.[128] Similar to baselines

---

124. 455 Pa. Super. 426, 688 A.2d 721 (1997).
125. 455 Pa. Super. 426, 428, 688 A.2d 721, 722 (1997).
126. 96 N.J. 538, 476 A. 2d 1219 (1984).
127. 96 N.J. 538, 558, 476 A. 2d 1219, 1229.
128. "To deal with uncertainty, judges rely on presumptions." Jack M. Beerman & Joseph William Singer, *Baseline Questions in Legal Reasoning:*

are "cognitive schemas," which are unexamined and often unspo-
ken assumptions about human potential that purport to explain
existing social relationships.[129] Both baselines and cognitive schemas
unconsciously affect how we view a legal problem.

In summary, tradition was the principal source of the common
law, and it remains a powerful if often invisible force in determining what the law is.

The Example of Property in Jobs, 23 GA. L. REV. 911, 933 (1989) (hereinafter *Baseline Questions*).

129. See Marianne LaFrance, *The Schemas and Schemes in Sex Discrimination*, 65 BROOK. L. REV. 1063 (1999) (showing how assumptions
about women have shaped the law); and Todd Brower,*"A Stranger to Its Laws:"
Homosexuality, Schemas, and the Lessons and Limits of Reasoning by Analogy*, 38 SANTA CLARA L. REV. 65 (1997) (dealing with assumptions about
gays).

CHAPTER 7

Policy

There is a fundamental difference between policy arguments and the other four types of legal argument. The distinctive feature of policy arguments is that they are consequentialist in nature. The other four types of argument are appeals to authority, but the core of a policy argument is that a certain interpretation of the law will bring about a certain state of affairs, and this state of affairs is either acceptable or unacceptable in the eyes of the law. Deriving rules of law from text, intent, precedent and tradition is inherently conventional; such rules represent specific choices that our lawgivers have already made. Deriving rules from policy arguments, on the other hand, is inherently open-ended; the specific choice has not yet been made. Text, intent, precedent and tradition look principally to the past for guidance; policy arguments look to the future for confirmation.

The difference between policy analysis and the other four types of legal arguments is analogous to the difference between "rules" and "standards." Primary rules of behavior may be stated in the form of rules or in the form of standards. A law imposing a speed limit of "65 miles per hour" is a rule. A law requiring that drivers proceed at a "reasonable rate of speed" is a standard. The application of a rule depends solely on the existence of specific facts (How fast was the car going?). The application of a standard involves the consideration of one or more facts in light of one or more underlying values (How fast was the car going, what were the weather and traffic conditions, and how much danger will the law tolerate?). A famous standard is Judge Learned Hand's[130] formula for determining liability

---

130. Learned Hand was, in the opinion of many, "one of the greatest

under the law of tort from the case of *United States v. Carroll Towing*.[131] *Carroll Towing* involved a barge that broke away from its moorings and damaged other vessels. Hand determined liability not by asking whether the defendant owed a preexisting "duty" to the plaintiff, but rather by creating a standard that balanced a number of consequentialist factors:

> Since there are occasions when every vessel will break from her moorings, and since, if she does, she becomes a menace to those about her; the owner's duty, as in other similar situations, to provide against resulting injuries is a function of three variables: (1) The probability that she will break away; (2) the gravity of the resulting injury, if she does; (3) the burden of adequate precautions.[132]

In *Dennis v. United States*,[133] Hand utilized the same formula to resolve a First Amendment problem. Hand did not attempt to determine, on an *a priori* basis, what the defendant's "natural rights" were. Instead, he measured the defendant's right to freedom of speech by reference to the harmful consequences that would result from allowing the speech. He said: "In each case [courts] must ask whether the gravity of the 'evil,' discounted by its improbability, justifies such invasion of free speech as is necessary to avoid the danger."[134]

---

judges in American history." John Wertheimer, *Book Review: Learned Hand: The Man and the Judge, by Gerald Gunther*, 14 Const. Comment. 236 (1997). Although never elevated to the United States Supreme Court, he served as a federal judge for over fifty years. For a thorough examination of his life and his influential judicial opinions see Gerald Gunther, Learned Hand: The Man and the Judge (1994).

131. 159 F.2d 169 (2nd Cir. 1947).
132. *Id.* at 173.
133. 183 F.2d 201 (1950), *aff'd* 341 U.S. 494 (1951).
134. *Id.* at 212. On appeal in *Dennis*, the United States Supreme Court adopted Hand's formula as expressing the meaning of the "clear and present danger" test. 341 U.S. 494, 510 (1951). The Supreme Court implicitly extended Hand's analysis to procedural due process cases in Mathews v. Eldridge, 424 U.S. 319 (1976). See Randy Lee, *Twenty-Five Years After*

Policy arguments are not identical to standards. Policy arguments are not primary rules of behavior, like speed limits, standards of tort liability, or interpretations of the First Amendment. Instead, policy arguments are used to *derive* rules of law, just as arguments based on text, intent, precedent, and tradition are used to derive rules of law. However, the analogy between policy arguments and standards is informative because both policy arguments and standards are concerned not with abstractions such as "duty" and "natural law," but with the *consequences* of interpreting the law in a particular manner. A policy argument construes the law not by consulting a dictionary, but by inquiring into the underlying *purposes* of the law. The meaning of the law is determined not by a literal definition of its terms, but by reference to the *values* that the law is intended to serve.

The remainder of this chapter relates how policy arguments came to be accepted as legal arguments, and describes the structure of policy arguments.

1. The History of Policy Arguments

Over the last century the method of legal reasoning called "policy analysis" or "legal realism"[135] took root in our jurisprudence and became the dominant force in American law.[136] Policy analy-

---

Goldberg v. Kelly: Traveling From the Right Spot on the Wrong Road to the Wrong Place, 23 Cap. U. L. Rev. 863, 894, 909 (1994).

135. Judge Richard Posner defines legal realism as "the use of policy analysis in legal reasoning." Richard Posner, *Jurisprudential Responses to Legal Realism*, 73 Cornell L. Rev. 326 (1988).

136. Cardozo said: "From history and philosophy and custom, we pass, therefore, to the force which in our day and generation is becoming the greatest of them all, the power of social justice which finds its power and expression in the method of sociology." Cardozo, The Nature of the Judicial Process, *supra* note 1, at 65–66. The history of the incorporation of policy analysis into American law is described in Morton J. Horwitz, The Transformation of American Law 1870–1960 169–246 (1992) (hereinafter Transformation 1870–1960).

sis grew out of the British school of utilitarianism and the American philosophy of pragmatism. It was introduced into our case law by the greatest American judges of the 20th Century: Learned Hand, Oliver Wendell Holmes, Louis Brandeis, and Benjamin Cardozo. This method of analysis was also written into our statutory law by noted reformers such as Grant Gilmore and Karl Llewellyn.

Policy analysis originated in the ancient philosophy of teleology developed by Aristotle. Aristotle started by identifying the purposes of human existence, and inferred from these purposes the general principles of right conduct.[137] Teleology is an "ends-means" philosophy, which for centuries was overshadowed by competing philosophies such as deontology and natural law. Deontologists such as Immanuel Kant taught that morality is grounded in "duty," and that our duties to each other can be deduced from fundamental and absolute principles ("categorical imperatives") that are derived from reason itself.[138] The similar belief in natural law rests upon the assumption that human laws should reflect fundamental principles that are either inherent in human nature or that are ordained by God.[139] As noted above, Learned Hand, in *Carroll Towing* and *Dennis*, rejected both duty and natural law in favor of a consequentialist analysis. What follows is a brief description of how teleology evolved into the policy analysis of American legal reasoning.

Teleology was revived in the 18th and 19th Centuries by the British political philosophers Jeremy Bentham and John Stuart Mill, who called their method of analysis "utilitarianism."[140] Their the-

---

137. ARISTOTLE, NICHOMACHEAN ETHICS 3 (Ostwald Trans. 1962).

138. A contemporary example of the Kantian, deontological approach to defining legal responsibility is JOHN RAWLS, A THEORY OF JUSTICE (1971). See George P. Fletcher, *Why Kant*, 87 COLUM. L. REV. 421, 428 (1987).

139. As such, "natural law" is an alternative to utilitarian analysis. *Id.* at 422. The leading contemporary work by a "natural lawyer" is JOHN FINNIS, NATURAL LAW AND NATURAL RIGHTS (1980).

140. Bentham introduced his theory of utility in INTRODUCTION TO PRINCIPLES OF MORALS AND LEGISLATION (1789), and John Stuart Mill systematized the philosophy of utilitarianism in his essay *Utilitarianism* published in 1863. 22 ENCYCLOPEDIA BRITANNICA 914 (1950). Sources that

sis was that laws and institutions should not be evaluated according to tradition nor according to *a priori* conceptions of "natural law" but rather in light of the *consequences* these laws and institutions bring about.[141]

The consequentialist analysis that was characteristic of utilitarian philosophy was incorporated into the philosophy of "pragmatism" developed by the 19th Century American philosopher Charles Sanders Peirce.[142] This method of thought was popularized at the turn of the century by William James, the author of *Pragmatism*.[143] However, American courts did not formally recognize consequen-

---

discuss the impact of utilitarian philosophy on legal realism and policy analysis include H. L. POHLMAN, JUSTICE OLIVER WENDELL HOLMES AND UTILITARIAN JURISPRUDENCE (1984) and Wilson Huhn, *Mill's Theory of Liberty in Constitutional Interpretation*, 22 AKRON L. REV. 133 (1988).

141. Jeremy Bentham expressed the following opinion about natural law: "All this talk about nature, natural rights, natural justice and injustice proves two things and two things only, the heat of passions and the darkness of understanding." JEREMY BENTHAM, THE LIMITS OF JURISPRUDENCE DEFINED 84 (Charles W. Everett ed., 1945).

142. Peirce introduced his theory of Pragmatism in Popular Science Monthly in January, 1878. 17 ENCYCLOPEDIA BRITANNICA 443 (1950). Peirce was member of the Metaphysical Club at Harvard, a circle that included Oliver Wendell Holmes. Catherine Wells Hantzis, *Legal Innovation Within the Wider Intellectual Tradition: The Pragmatism of Oliver Wendell Holmes, Jr.*, 82 Nw. U. L. REV. 541 (1988). For a discussion of the impact of Pragmatism on American legal thought *see* Roberta Kevelson, *Semiotics and Methods of Legal Inquiry: Interpretation and Discovery in Law from the Perspective of Peirce's Speculative Rhetoric*, 61 IND. L. J. 355, 356 (1986) (tracing legal realism to the pragmatic philosophy of Charles Sanders Peirce). *See generally* Grey, *Holmes and Legal Pragmatism, supra* note 10.

143. WILLIAM JAMES, PRAGMATISM: A NEW NAME FOR OLD WAYS OF THINKING (1907). William James "showed how the meaning of any idea whatsoever — scientific, religious, philosophical, political, social, personal — can be found ultimately in nothing save the succession of experiential consequences it lead through and to, that truth and error are identical with these consequences or else nothing with reach of the mind at all." 12 ENCYCLOPEDIA BRITANNICA 884 (1950). Learned Hand was a student of William James at Harvard. Wertheimer, *supra* note 130, at 237.

tialist analysis as a legitimate *legal* argument until the "legal realism" movement in the first half of the 20th century.[144]

Just as utilitarianism sought to supplant deontology in philosophical circles, in the field of law policy analysis struggled against the "categorical thinking" of the 19th Century.[145] As noted in Chapter 1, the traditional view of law was that it was a science, a view that culminated in the teaching of Christopher Columbus Langdell. In his casebook on contracts, Langdell conceived of law as a set of principles or doctrines that exist independently of human intention, and that can be discovered through diligent study. Langdell wrote:

> Law, considered as a science, consists of certain principles or doctrines. To have such a mastery of these as to

---

144. Despite the fact that consequentialist reasoning was denied formal recognition as legal argument, its use was not unknown to nineteenth century courts. For example, in State v. Post, 20 N.J.L. 368 (1845), the court, in considering whether slavery had been abolished by the state constitution, described the hardships that would befall elderly and infirm slaves if masters were relieved of their responsibility to support them, and then noted that "these consequences, while they can have no legitimate influence upon the decision of the question, nevertheless give it more than ordinary importance, and call for our most serious and anxious consideration." *Id.* at 372. Craig Evan Klafter traces the origin of consequentialist analysis in American law to the early years of the Republic:

> During America's post-Revolutionary and early National periods, [legal] educators — aided by thousands of their students who quickly assumed most prominent positions in the Bar successfully — encouraged jurists to redact into American legal practice a modified doctrine of *stare decisis* which provided that precedents established by American courts should be strictly adhered to while permitting English precedents to be questioned against the standards of utility, logic, morality, and such conflicting American law and policy as already existed....

Craig Evan Klafter, Reason Over Precedents: Origins of American Legal Thought 3 (1993). *See also* Chapter One of Horwitz, The Transformation of American Law 1780–1860, at 1–30 (1977), entitled *The Emergence of an Instrumental Conception of Law.*

145. Horwitz, Transformation 1870–1960, *supra* note 136, at 199.

be able to apply them with constant facility and certainty to the ever-tangled skein of human affairs, is what constitutes a true lawyer; and hence to acquire that mastery should be the business of every earnest student of law.[146]

Grant Gilmore[147] summarized Langdell's view of law as science in these words: "The basic idea of the Langdellian revolution seems to have been that there really is such a thing as the one true rule of law, universal and unchanging, always and everywhere the same —a sort of mystical absolute."[148] Gilmore added, "To all of us, I dare say, the idea seems absurd."[149]

During the first half of the 20th Century Langdell's idealist vision of the law, which identified law with science and mathematics, was challenged and eventually overcome by the competing philosophy of legal realism. The legal realists rebelled against the formalism of the 19th century and insisted that the law be analyzed in light of its purposes and likely consequences, rather than as an exercise in deductive logic.

Leading the charge on Langdell's vision of law as science was Oliver Wendell Holmes. Holmes, reviewing Langdell's casebook in

---

146. CHRISTOPHER LANGDELL, A SELECTION OF CASES ON THE LAW OF CONTRACTS vi (1871).

147. Gilmore drafted Article 9 of the Uniform Commercial Code, which has been called "perhaps the largest burst of legal creativity in modern commercial law." William J. Woodward, Jr., *The Realist and Secured Credit: Grant Gilmore, Common-Law Courts, and the Article 9 Reform Process*, 82 CORNELL L. REV. 1511, 1519, 1521 (1997). Gilmore also authored the classic realist work THE DEATH OF CONTRACT (1974).

148. GRANT GILMORE, THE DEATH OF CONTRACT 97–98 (1974) (footnote omitted).

149. *Id.* at 98. Gilmore's objection to legal formalism as "universal and unchanging" is consistent with H.L.A. Hart's observation that the weakness of legal formalism was not its reliance upon logic, but its failure to acknowledge the "open texture" (ambiguity) of legal rules. See Douglas Lind, *Logic, Intuition, and the Positivist Legacy of H.L.A. Hart*, 52 SMU L. REV. 135, 152–157 (1999).

1880, characterized Langdell as a "legal theologian,"[150] and launched
a spirited attack on the notion of law as science. Holmes had previously disputed the proposition that rules of law could be derived
by deduction:

> In form [the] growth [of the law] is logical. The official
> theory is that each new decision follows syllogistically
> from existing precedents.... On the other hand, in sub-
> stance the growth of the law is legislative.... Every im-
> portant principle which is developed by litigation is in
> fact and at bottom the result of more or less definitely
> understood views of public policy.... [151]

"Legal realists" like Holmes rejected the idealists' view of law as
science. In 1929, John Dickinson of Princeton explained why law
is not a science:

> [J]ural laws are not, like scientific "laws," descriptive
> statements of verifiable relations between persons or

150. Oliver Wendell Holmes, *Book Notices*, 14 AM. LAW. 233, 234
(1880). In a similar spirit Grant Gilmore criticized Langdell's conceptu-
alism, GRANT GILMORE, THE AGES OF AMERICAN LAW 42–48 (1977), while
Richard Posner calls Langdell's approach "Platonism." Richard Posner, *The
Decline of Law as an Autonomous Discipline*, 100 HARV. L. REV. 761, 762
(1987). In contrast, Marcia Speziale persuasively argues that Langdell was
not a formalist, but rather that by reforming the teaching of law from the
preaching of doctrine to the study of cases, he laid the groundwork for
the realistic revolution in law. Speziale, *supra* note 12, at 3–4. She suggests that Langdell's methods were empirical and inductive, not deductive, and that this signaled a movement away from the notion of law as
an absolute canon of doctrine. *Id.* at 3. Speziale's view of Langdell was
shared by Roscoe Pound, who said, "Langdell was always worried about
'Why' and 'How?' He didn't care particularly whether you knew a rule or
could state the rule or not, but how did the court do this? And why did it
do it? That was his approach all the time." ROBERT STEVENS, LAW SCHOOL:
LEGAL EDUCATION IN AMERICA FROM THE 1850S TO THE 1950S 55 (1983).
151. Oliver Wendell Holmes, *Common Carriers and the Common Law*,
13 AM. L. REV. 609, 631 (1879).

things—relations which exist and will continue to exist irrespective of whether human choice and agency enter into the situation.... They are consequently the result of value-judgments, rather than of judgments of fact— judgments, i.e., that one arrangement of relations is better, as for some reason more just or more convenient, than another arrangement which is admitted to be physically possible.[152]

The central point of Oliver Wendell Holmes' 1897 masterpiece, *The Path of the Law*, was that courts ought to base their decisions upon "rational policy" rather than "tradition."[153] He debunked the notion that a system of law "can be worked out like mathematics from some general axioms of conduct,"[154] and he admonished legal educators to teach policy analysis:

I cannot but believe that if the training of lawyers led them habitually to consider more definitely and explicitly the social advantage on which the rule they lay down must be justified, they sometimes would hesitate where now they are confident, and see that really they were taking sides upon debatable and often burning questions.[155]

Over the course of his career Holmes repeatedly returned to this topic, and many of his famous aphorisms echo this theme. In 1905, in his *Lochner* dissent, Holmes wrote, "General propositions do

---

152. John Dickinson, *The Law Behind Law II*, 29 COLUM. L. REV. 285, 289–290 (1929). Philip Bobbitt has persuasively made this same point. Bobbitt contends that many people make the "fundamental epistemological mistake" of assuming "that law-statements are statements about the world (like the statements of science) and thus must be verified by a correspondence with facts about the world." PHILIP BOBBITT, CONSTITUTIONAL INTERPRETATION, *supra* note 2, at xii. Bobbitt suggests that law is not a science, but "something we do." *Id.* at 24.
153. Holmes, *Path*, *supra* note 19, at 1004.
154. *Id.* at 998.
155. *Id.* at 1000.

not decide concrete cases,"[156] and in 1921 he noted, "A page of history is worth a volume of logic."[157]

In the early 20th Century another leading figure in American legal education took up the same banner. Roscoe Pound, Dean of Harvard Law School, used the term "sociological jurisprudence" to describe this new method of analysis.[158] Pound insisted that in interpreting the law judges should "take more account, and more intelligent account, of the social facts upon which law must proceed and to which it is to be applied."[159]

Karl Llewellyn, a principal drafter of the Uniform Commercial Code, described sociological jurisprudence in the following terms:

> [T]he central problem of all law has to do with this still almost completely neglected descriptive science, with this "legal sociology," this natural science of living law. What we need to study, what we must know, is not how a legal rule reads, nor how a philosophically correct rule would read, but what the legal rule means. Not in... the heaven of legal concepts, but in human experience. What happens in life with it? What does a law mean to ordinary people?[160]

---

156. Lochner v. New York, 198 U.S. 45, 75 (1905) (Holmes, J. dissenting).

157. New York Trust Company v. Eisner, 256 U.S. 345, 349 (1921).

158. Roscoe Pound, *The Scope and Purpose of Sociological Jurisprudence, Part 3*, 25 HARV. L. REV. 489 (1912).

159. *Id.* Pound's emphasis on results and "social science" is in contrast to Langdell's understanding of law as a set of immutable principles. See Wai Chee Dimock, *Rules of Law, Laws of Science*, 13 YALE J.L. & HUMAN. 203, 213–218 (2001), for an extended discussion of Pound's understanding of the scientific nature of law.

160. Michael Ansaldi, *The German Llewellyn*, 58 BROOK. L. REV. 705, 748–749 (1992). Llewellyn's contribution to the legal realism movement is described in WILLIAM TWINING, KARL LLEWELLYN AND THE REALIST MOVEMENT (1973); and William Twining, *Talk about Realism*, 60 N.Y.U. L. Rev. 329, 342 (1985). Llewellyn's influence on the Uniform Commercial Code is the subject of Ingrid Michelsen Hillinger, *The Article 2 Mer-*

Louis Brandeis,[161] Holmes' colleague on the Supreme Court and another founder of the school of legal realism, agreed with Pound and Llewellyn that judges should focus on the facts of the case, rather than on general principles: "In the past the courts have reached their conclusions largely deductively from preconceived notions and precedents. The method I have tried to employ in arguing cases before them has been inductive, reasoning from the facts."[162]

This method of legal reasoning became known as "legal realism," as distinguished from the "idealist" vision of law that was held by Langdell and the formalists of the 19th Century. The legal realists were skeptical, not nihilistic. They did not equate law with power, nor did they consider legal reasoning to be a mask to cover the unprincipled exercise of power.[163] Instead, they constructed an

chant Rules: Karl Llewellyn's Attempt to Achieve the Good, the True, the Beautiful in Commercial Law, 73 Geo. L.J. 1141 (1985); and Charles A. Bane, From Holt and Mansfield to Story to Llewellyn and Mentschikoff: The Progressive Development of Commercial Law, 37 U. Miami L. Rev. 351 (1983).

161. Louis Brandeis, as an attorney, fought for social progress, and as a justice of the United States Supreme Court he fervently defended social and political rights. See Philippa Strum, Louis D. Brandeis: Justice for the People (1984). Like Holmes, Brandeis elevated "experience" over "logic." Schwartz, supra note 55, at 214–216. The development of the "Brandeis brief" that incorporated studies from social science is discussed in the text accompanying notes 176–177 infra.

162. Solomon Goldman, The Words of Justice Brandeis 77 (1953).

163. Legal Realism may be distinguished from Critical Legal Studies, "the more ambitious descendent of legal realism," which contends that "[a]ll legal texts, theories, arguments, and positions are radically contextual in nature, and legal reasons are merely ad hoc or post hoc rationalizations for prior 'situated' beliefs." C.J. Summers, Distorting Reason, 11 Yale J.L. & Human. 529 (1999) (critiquing Pierre Schlag, The Enchantment of Reason (1998)). Schlag, a proponent of critical legal studies, suggests that reason in legal analysis is an illusion. Id. Summers concludes that the issues raised by critical legal theorists "are serious and worthy of study," but that "[c]ritical theorists have done them a disservice by substituting trendy jargon, impressionistic arguments, and attacks on the status quo

alternative method to interpret the law through balancing and policy analysis.[164] Justice Cardozo did not reject deductive logic and
traditional methods of legal reasoning, but he did find them to be
incomplete:

> The final cause of law is the welfare of society. The rule
> that misses its aim cannot permanently justify its exis-
> tence.... Logic and history and custom have their place.
> We will shape the law to conform to them when we may;
> but only within bounds. The end which the law serves
> will dominate them all.[165]

Legal realism replaced formalism and became the dominant force
in American law because it is a more complete and more satisfying
approach to solving hard legal problems. A fundamental aim of legal
realism was, as Holmes observed, "to get the dragon out of his cave."
Holmes said, "When you get the dragon out of his cave on to the
plain and into the daylight, you can count his teeth and claws, and
see just what is his strength."[166] By this Holmes meant that judges
should discuss the real reasons for their opinions—how their interpretations of the law would affect society. H.L.A. Hart echoed Holmes:
"[J]udges should not seek to bootleg silently into the law their own
conceptions of the law's aims or justice or social policy or other extra-

---

for careful argumentation, attention to detail, charitable consideration of
competing positions, and intellectual humility." *Id.* at 539.

164. Morton Horwitz contrasts the standard legal thinking of the 19th
and 20th centuries:

> Contemporary thinkers typically have been engaged in balanc-
> ing conflicting policies and "drawing lines" somewhere between
> them. Nineteenth-century categorizing typically sought to demon-
> strate "differences of kind" among legal classifications; twenti-
> eth-century balancing tests deal only with "differences of degree."

Horwitz, Transformation 1870–1960, *supra* note 136, at 17.

165. Cardozo, The Nature of the Judicial Process, *supra* note 1,
at 66.

166. Holmes, *Path, supra* note 19, at 1001.

legal elements required for decision, but should openly identify and discuss them."[167]

The legal realists wanted the courts to expose the underlying policies of the law so as not to hide the true rationale of a decision behind a formalistic analysis.[168] The disclosure of the true reasons for a decision performs a valuable function: the stated premises of the law will over time be empirically tested,[169] and as a result, unfounded assumptions and improper purposes will be exposed.

2. The Structure of Policy Arguments

Policy analysis proceeds in two steps. Every policy argument consists of a predictive statement and an evaluative judgment. The court first predicts the consequences that will flow from giving the law one interpretation or another, and then decides which set of consequences is more consistent with the underlying values of the law.

---

167. H.L.A. Hart, Essays in Jurisprudence and Philosophy 130–132 (1983).

168. Holmes explained: "I think that the judges themselves have failed adequately to recognize their duty of weighing considerations of social advantage. The duty is inevitable, and the result of the often proclaimed judicial aversion to deal with such considerations is simply to leave the very ground and foundation of judgments inarticulate, and often unconscious...." Holmes, *Path, supra* note 19, at 999.

169. For example, in Erickson v. Erickson, 246 Conn. 359, 716 A.2D 92 (Conn. 1998), the Connecticut Supreme Court overruled precedent and held that extrinsic evidence of a testator's intent is admissible in cases where that intent was thwarted by a "scrivener's error." 246 Conn. at 371, 716 A.2d at 98, (overruling Connecticut Junior Republic v. Sharon Hospital, 188 Conn. 1, 448 A.2d 190 (1982)). The majority in *Erickson* observed that "[e]xperience can and often does demonstrate that a rule, once believed sound, needs modification to serve justice better." 246 Conn. at 372, 716 A.2d at 99, (internal quotations and citations omitted). The *Ericson* court explicitly adopted the policy analysis of the dissent from *Connecticut Junior Republic*. 246 Conn. at 373–375, 716 A.2d at 99–100.

a. The Predictive Statement

How does a court take the first step in creating a policy argument? What is the evidence that a court uses to make the factual prediction of the consequences that will flow from its interpretation of the law? In making this determination the courts are not limited to evidence that is presented by the parties at trial. Although the first step of a policy argument requires the court to make a factual determination, this is not a "question of fact" that is determined by a jury or by a judge sitting as a "trier of fact." Instead, the factual basis for a policy argument presents a "question of law" to be determined solely by the judge. On appeal, judicial review of the factual basis for a policy argument is not limited to the evidence in the record, but may be determined *de novo* by the appellate court on the basis of information that is presented to the court for the first time on appeal.

Perhaps the most famous policy argument by an American court is that found in the case of *Brown v. Board of Education*,[170] in which the court struck down state-sponsored racial segregation of public schools. The factual prediction supporting the court's policy argument was that enforced segregation of the races harms children, and "may affect their hearts and minds in a way unlikely ever to be undone."[171] In support of this conclusion the Supreme Court of the United States cited seven books and articles by social scientists.[172] The Supreme Court took judicial notice of the truth of the factual assertion that segregation is harmful.

---

170. 347 U.S. 483 (1954).

171. *Id.* at 494.

172. *Id.* at 494, fn. 11. Some scholars support the court's judicial factfinding in Brown, and some object to it. Compare Richard L. Aynes, *An Examination of Brown in Light of Plessy and Croson: Lessons for the 1990s*, 7 Harv. Blackletter J. 149, 152–153 (1990) (defending footnote 11) with Donald N. Bersoff and David J. Glass, *The Not-So Weisman: The Supreme Court's Continuing Misuse of Social Science Research*, 2 U. Chi. L. Sch. Roundtable 279, 293–294 (1995) (criticizing footnote 11).

Judicial notice of the factual basis for a policy argument is different from judicial notice of questions of fact. Judicial notice of questions of fact at trial is governed by Evidence Rule 201, entitled "Judicial Notice of Adjudicative Facts." Under Rule 201 courts are permitted to take judicial notice of facts that would otherwise be decided by the trier of fact only if the facts are "generally known" or "capable of accurate and ready determination by resort to sources whose accuracy cannot reasonably be questioned."[173] For example, under Evidence Rule 201 a judge could take judicial notice of the time that the sun set on a particular date in a trial where that was a material fact.

In contrast, the validity of a policy argument does not present a question of adjudicative fact to be determined by a jury, and our terminology reflects this difference. The factual premise of a policy argument is referred to as "legislative fact" to be determined by the court as a matter of law, as contrasted to questions of "adjudicative fact" to be determined by a jury.[174] Judicial notice of "legislative facts" is not subject to the limitations of Rule 201 or any other rule of evidence.[175]

Accordingly, when taking judicial notice of the factual basis of a policy argument a trial or appellate court is not limited to evidence that is introduced by the parties at trial, it is not limited to facts that are generally known, and it is not limited to facts that are set forth in sources of unquestioned accuracy. Rather, the court may take judicial notice of any "legislative facts" that have been brought to its attention by the parties in oral argument or in a brief.

A brief that sets forth substantial evidence of "legislative facts" supporting a policy argument is called a "Brandeis brief" after the

---

173. Fed. Evid. R. 201(b).

174. The distinction between "legislative facts" and "adjudicative facts" was first described by Kenneth Culp Davis in *An Approach to Problems of Evidence in the Administrative Process*, 55 Harv. L. Rev. 364, 404–407 (1942).

175. *See* the Advisory Committee Notes to Federal Evidence Rule 201.

brief that Louis Brandeis submitted to the United States Supreme
Court in *Muller v. Oregon*.[176] In *Muller* Brandeis was defending the
constitutionality of an Oregon statute establishing maximum hours
of work for women. Brandeis submitted a brief summarizing over
ninety reports and studies supporting the beneficial effect of maximum hour legislation on working women and their families, under
the heading *The World's Experience Upon Which the Legislation Limiting the Hours of Labor for Women Is Based*.[177]

Even when the parties fail to adduce any proof concerning the
underlying policies of the law, the court is free to undertake an independent judicial inquiry into the underlying facts which bear
upon the policy choice. In *United States v. Carolene Products*,[178] the
Supreme Court held: "Where the existence of a rational basis for legislation [depends] upon facts beyond the sphere of judicial notice,
such facts may properly be made the subject of judicial inquiry."[179]

Policy analysis differs from the other four types of legal arguments in that the scope of information that the court may draw on
is virtually unlimited. When a court makes an argument based
upon text, intent, precedent, or tradition, it is attempting to determine
the policy choice that has already been made by others. Proof of
this choice is necessarily limited to specific sources of information.
In contrast, policy analysis invites the court itself to make a policy
choice by balancing all of the relevant values and interests that will
be affected by the decision to pursue a particular policy, and the
court has free rein to assemble the evidence that would support its
policy judgment.

---

176. 208 U.S. 412 (1908).

177. The original "Brandeis brief" is reproduced at 16 Landmark
Briefs and Arguments of the Supreme Court of the United States:
Constitutional Law 63–113 (Philip B. Kurland & Gerhard Casper, eds.
1975). For a discussion of the brief and its significance *see* Paul L. Rosen,
The Supreme Court and Social Science 75–87 (1972).

178. 304 U.S. 144 (1938).

179. *Id.* at 153.

b. The Evaluative Judgment

Once a court has predicted how a proposed interpretation of the law will affect society, it must then proceed to determine whether or not these consequences are acceptable or unacceptable. This judgment requires the court to articulate the underlying purposes of the law, which is often difficult and controversial. For example, is the sole purpose of the law of contract to enforce promises that are supported by adequate consideration? Legal scholars and judges who adhere to the school of "law and economics" maintain that promisekeeping is not the only goal of contract law. They contend that there is also a competing goal of maximizing the efficient operation of the market. Professor James Robinson articulates the "law and economics" position: "This notion that parties must always live up to their promises regardless of the cost of doing so is at odds with contract law's fundamental economic, nonpunitive view of contract breachers."[180]

Judge Richard Posner, a leading figure of the school of law and economics, has argued that even freedom of speech may be understood from an economic perspective.[181] Judge Posner has also pointed out that different people read a variety of policy goals into the Constitution:

> When you think of all those constitutional theories jostling one another—Epstein's that would repeal the New Deal, Ackerman's and Sunstein's that would constitutionalize it, Michelman's that would constitutionalize the platform of the Democratic Party, Tushnet's that would make the Constitution a charter of socialism, Ely's that would resurrect Earl Warren, and some that would mold constitutional law to the Thomists' version

---

180. F. James Robinson, *If Wishes Were Horses: The Economic-Waste Doctrine in Construction Litigation*, 70 APR J. Kan. B.A. 34 (2001).

181. *See* Richard A. Posner, *Free Speech in an Economic Perspective*, 20 Suffolk L. Rev. 1 (1986).

of natural law—you see the range of choice that the approach legitimizes and, as a result, the instability of constitutional doctrine that it portends.[182]

It is because of the indeterminacy created by the selection of policy goals that Robert Bork considers policy analysis to be an "illegitimate" form of argument in the interpretation of the Constitution.[183] In Bork's opinion, the Supreme Court has, in dozens of cases, "without authority in the Constitution...forced Americans to adopt the Court's view of morality rather than their own."[184]

Another source of indeterminacy that is inherent to policy arguments is the process of balancing. This balancing process is illustrated by the decision of the New Jersey Supreme Court in *Unico v. Owen*,[185] a contracts case where the court invoked the principle of "unconscionability." In deciding whether to give effect to a contractual provision that forced the buyer to pay for goods even if they were defective or if they were never delivered, the New Jersey Supreme Court balanced the interests of the commercial community against the interests of installment buyers:

> The courts have recognized that the basic problem in consumer goods sales and financing is that of balancing the interest of the commercial community in unrestricted negotiability of commercial paper against the interest of installment buyers of such goods in the preservation of their normal remedy of withholding payment when, as in this case, the seller fails to deliver as agreed, and thus the consideration for his obligation fails.[186]

182. Richard Posner, *Legal Reasoning from the Top Down and from the Bottom Up: The Question of Unenumerated Constitutional Rights*, 59 U. Chi. L. Rev. 433 (1992).
183. Bork, *Neutral Principles, supra* note 64, at 6.
184. Robert H. Bork, Slouching Towards Gomorrah 114 (1996).
185. 50 N.J. 101, 232 A. 2d 405 (1967).
186. *Id.* at 112, 232 A.2d 405, 411.

In summary, policy arguments are consequentialist arguments that consist of a predictive statement and an evaluative judgment. The predictive statement may be supported by judicial notice of "legislative facts." The evaluative judgment requires the court to determine the values that are served by the law, and may also require the court to balance competing values.

CHAPTER 8

Identifying the Five Types
of Legal Arguments

The first step in the process of mastering the five types of legal arguments is to learn to identify each type of argument. To assist you in learning this skill I have presented excerpts from *People v. Gibbons*, a criminal case where a California appellate court interpreted the state's Privacy Act. In *Gibbons*, the defendant had videotaped his own sexual encounters with women who were unaware that they were being recorded, and he was charged with violating the California Privacy Act, which made it illegal to record "confidential communications" without the consent of all of the parties to the communication. Gibbons was convicted by a jury. Reprinted below are excerpts from the opinions written by judges of the state court that heard his appeal from that conviction. Judge Hollenhurst wrote the opinion for the majority affirming Gibbons' conviction, while Judge Campbell dissented. Each type of legal argument in their opinions is labeled in the margin.

PEOPLE V. GIBBONS, 215 Cal.App.3d 1204, 263 Cal.Rptr. 905 (4th Dist. 1989)

HOLLENHORST, Associate Justice.

In this appeal, we are asked for the first time to decide whether the surreptitious videotaping of sexual activity violates California's privacy statutes, Penal Code sections 630 and 632. The trial court overruled defendant's demurrer and a jury convicted defendant. Defendant appeals arguing the conduct in question is not prohibited by these sections. We agree with the trial court's determination and affirm.

FACTS

On three different occasions, defendant invited young women to his residence. In the bedroom, with the door closed and window curtains drawn, defendant and the three women engaged in sexual activity including sexual intercourse. Without obtaining the consent of the women, defendant videotaped these encounters utilizing a video camera which he had hidden in the closet. The women were never advised of the existence of the camera until being subsequently informed by police who recovered the videotapes.

DISCUSSION

Penal Code sections 630 and 632 define the purpose of the privacy act and its proscriptions. Neither side has provided controlling authority dealing directly with videotaping; however, as we discuss, the language of the statute and cases make it clear that the legislature intended to control the activity underlying this case.

The purpose of the statutes is clear and unambiguous. Initially, in section 630, the legislature recognized that technology had advanced to the extent that privacy could be imperiled unless the legislature intervened. The privacy statutes were enacted after a series of hodgepodge regulations dealing with privacy in communications had been amended and reamended. It was out of recognition that the entire privacy area needed overhaul that the privacy statutes were adopted. (Van Boven, *Electronic Surveillance in California: A Study in State Legislative Control* (1969) 57 Cal.L.Rev. 1182, 1189–1190.) We note in the text of section 630, no reference is made to a specific device or instrument for eavesdropping. Rather, the prohibition is based on the purpose for which the device or instrument is used. In section 632, the statute provides against the use of "any electronic amplifying or recording device" for the purpose of eavesdropping or recording private communications. We find that a video recorder is an instrument which, if used in manner

Text and Precedent

Intent

Text and Policy

Intent

Text

proscribed under section 632, is a recording device for purposes
of the privacy act. "If the words of the statute are clear, the court
should not add to or alter them to accomplish a purpose that does
not appear on the face of statute or from its legislative history."
(*People v. Knowles* (1950) 35 Cal.2d 175, 183, 217 P.2d 1.) "The
dominant objective of the act, as reflected in its preamble, is 'to
protect the right of privacy of the people of this state.'" (*Warden v.
Kahn* (1979) 99 Cal.App.3d 805, 810, 160 Cal.Rptr. 471.)

Text — Text, Precedent, and Policy

Defendant contends that even if a video recorder is a device or
instrument covered by the privacy act, the statute only prohibits the
surreptitious recording of oral communications, i.e., conversations,
and does not extend to the recording of sexual acts or other forms
of communication. We disagree. While communication and conversation are similar in their meaning, conversation refers to a *spo-
ken* exchange of thoughts, opinions, and feelings while communication
refers more broadly to the exchange of thoughts, messages or information by any means. (The American Heritage Dictionary (2d College ed. 1976) pp. 299, 320.)

Text

In other contexts, communication has been recognized to include not only oral or written communication but communication
by conduct as well. For example, in the area of attorney-client privilege, it has been recognized that "[t]he privilege embraces not only
oral or written statements but actions, signs, or other means of
communicating information by a client to his attorney. [Citations.]
'[A]lmost any act, done by the client in the sight of the attorney
and during the consultation, may conceivably be done by the client
as the subject of a communication, and the only question will be
whether, in the circumstances of the case, it was intended to be
done as such.'" (*City & County of S.F. v. Superior Court* (1951) 37
Cal.2d 227, 235–236, 231 P.2d 26.) That sexual relations is a form
of communication, be it communication of love, simple affection,
or, simply of oneself, cannot be readily disputed.**

Precedent

** The dissent contends that, *unlike other conduct such
as flag burning,* sexual conduct is not communication
because the message being conveyed by sexual conduct

Text

Text

is often difficult to decipher or understand. Implicit in this contention is the concession that communication is not limited to conversations and that at least *some* conduct is included in its definition. The suggestion, however, that "communication" should be limited to only those communications which are understood, be they words *or* conduct, is not only a strained construction of the word but one without support as well.

Intent

The statute is not limited to effective communication and we cannot believe the legislature would intend such a restriction. Just as the dissent recognizes that words can often be used to conceal rather than convey information, it can be said that people "hear" what they want to "hear." To attempt to define communication

Policy

by whether the message conveyed is accurately received would lead to absurd results.

Text

We acknowledge that certain terms used in the privacy act, such as "eavesdropping," "amplifying device" and "telephone," might suggest a narrow definition of communication, synonymous with conversation. However, section 630 expressly states the intent of the

Intent

legislature to protect the right of privacy of the people of this state. Consistent with the express declaration of intent and in the absence of any express statutory limitations, we find that "communication" as used in the privacy act is not limited to conversations or oral communications but rather encompasses any communication, re-

Text

gardless of its form, where any party to the communication desires it to be confined to the parties thereto. If the act covers eavesdropping on or recording of a telephone call, it surely covers the non-consensual recording of the most intimate and private form of communication between two people.

* * *

Precedent

[I]n *People v. Sobiek*, (1973) 30 Cal.App.3d 458, 473–475, 106 Cal. Rptr. 519, the court found no due process violation in applying the grand theft statute to a partner for the wrongful taking of partnership property even though dicta in prior decisions suggested otherwise.

Precedent

* * *

"The criterion in such cases is to examine whether common social duty would, under the circumstances, have suggested a more circumspect conduct." (People v. Sobiek).

Tradition and Precedent

DISPOSITION

Judgment is affirmed.

CAMPBELL, Presiding Justice, dissenting.

I disagree with the majority's strained construction of Penal Code section 632, and therefore dissent.

Neither language, nor legislative intent, nor case law supports the majority's construction of the term "communication."

Text, Intent and Precedent

The statutory language gives a defendant fair notice that the defendant's acts violated a statute as long as the language is construed "according to the fair import of [its] terms" not going "so far as to create an offense…by giving the terms used…unusual meanings."

Text

(*People v. Keeler, supra,* 2 Cal.3d at p. 632, 87 Cal.Rptr. 481, 470 P.2d 617.) "Penal statutes will not be made to reach beyond their plain intent; they include only those offenses coming clearly within the import of their language." (*Ibid.*)

Precedent
Text
Precedent

The majority holds that sexual conduct is a form of communication in the sense that it conveys the thoughts and emotions of the participants. This strained construction of "communication" attributes to that term the "unusual meaning" of sexual conduct, a meaning which does not come "clearly within the import" of communication. Sexual acts are *not* the *communication* of thoughts and feelings; rather, they are *evidence* of feelings in the same way that a deadly assault is evidence, not communication, of malice.

Text

To be distinguished from complex acts with multiple purposes in addition to communication, such as sexual conduct, are simple gestures and symbolic acts which have culturally determined meanings. Such acts as an affirmative nod and burning the flag are solely communicative in purpose in exactly the same sense as words or semaphore. The actor and observer are not so intent on the performance of these acts as on their meaning. The same cannot be said of more complex activities such as sexual conduct where multifarious purposes other than communication may be present exclusively, or concurrently and in varying degree, in any one instance, such as pleasure, procreation, and the satisfaction of a host of psychological, spiritual, and emotional needs and desires.

Text

Thus, when one thinks of communication, one does not ordinarily or usually think of sexual conduct because sex has so many other meanings and communication has more obvious and concrete associations all associated with words, gestures, and symbols. Sexual conduct is not exclusively, nor even primarily or usually, communication in the sense that words, gestures, and symbolic acts are exclusively communication; therefore, the plain and ordinary meaning of communication cannot include sexual conduct, and the majority's construction to that effect is strained and assigns an "unusual" meaning to communication not "clearly with the import" of that term. Although recording sexual conduct might be considered "within the reason or mischief" and "of equal atrocity, or of kindred character" with the recording of a confidential communication, that is not sufficient to construe communication to include sexual acts. It is not the function of this court "to fill an asserted 'gap' in the law" by punishing the recording of private sexual conduct when the Legislature has not clearly done so. (*Keeler*

Precedent

v. Superior Court, supra, 2 Cal.3d at p. 632–633, 87 Cal.Rptr. 481, 470 P.2d 617.)

In making this distinction between sex and communication, I recognize the unavoidable overlap of words and concepts at their margins which sometimes makes statutory construction an inexact process which is, perhaps, more of an art than a science. Indeed, I do not ignore that the oral communication, "I hate you," is evidence of a killer's malice just as is the assault, or that the sexual act

Text

does in a sense "communicate" affection. I do not mean that communication and evidence or communication and sex are mutually exclusive sets in a rigorous, mathematical sense. We figuratively say, "Acts speak louder than words."

However, an act communicates better than words, and sex is communication, only in the limited sense that sometimes the inferences to be drawn from acts are very clear, often because the actor was not intent upon restricting the inferences that could be drawn from his or her acts, whereas the actor can so easily lie with words. The point is that when a legislature uses a word in a penal statute, unless the legislative history indicates otherwise, it is not speaking figuratively by poetic images, allegory, and figures of speech. Rather, the legislature seeks to express the will of the people in direct, concrete, plain terms, not relying on peripheral meanings and innuendo when dealing with such a serious subject as the life and liberty of its citizens. Sexual conduct is not a direct, concrete, plain meaning of the term "communication;" we speak figuratively, poetically, romantically when we say that sexual intimacy communicates the thoughts and feelings of one for another.

In the context of this case, the legislative use of the plain and ordinary meaning of words means using the most general and unrestricted terms when it desires a broadly inclusive reading. The judiciary has recognized this legislative practice by the general rule of construction that the statutory construction most favorable to the defendant [generally the least inclusive] will be used when the statute is reasonably susceptible of two interpretations and legislative intent does not point to one of them. (*People v. Alday* (1973) 10 Cal.3d 392, 394–395, 110 Cal.Rptr. 617, 515 P.2d 1169.)

Thus, the majority is wrong in saying that the Legislature would have said "conversation" if they meant to preclude sexual conduct. If the Legislature had intended to reach the recording of private sexual conduct it would have used a term such as "confidential activity," an unmistakeably broad and all inclusive term, not "confidential communication," as it did, which only includes sexual intimacy in an unusual, nonliteral, figurative sense. It cannot reasonably be held that the Legislature intended by the use of the term "communication" to lead us into the fog shrouded maze of the mind's associations connected with one of humanity's most fundamental, complex, and poorly understood drives.

Having decided that the language of the statute does not sup-

Intent

port the majority's construction, I turn to other evidence of legislative intent recognizing that "'There are limits to this freedom to tamper with statutory language ... [.] The primary source of the legislative intent and purpose is in the words used; if these are clear the court should not seek hidden motive or objects which do not appear on the face of the statute or from its legislative history.' [Citation.]" (*Holder v. Superior Court* (1969) 269 Cal.App.2d 314, 318,

Precedent

74 Cal.Rptr. 853.) Contrary to the majority's holding, the above

Text

discussion justifies the holding that the term "communication" clearly does not embrace sexual conduct. We find no contrary indication in the legislative history which this court has examined consisting of the documents in the California State Archives concerning Assembly Bill 860 passed in 1967. (Stats.1967, ch. 1509, pp. 3584–3591.)

Former sections 653i and 653j, repealed in 1967 by AB 860, are the predecessors of section 632. (Stats.1967, ch. 1509, §§ 8, 9, p. 3589.) Section 653i, characterized by the Legislature as "relating to eavesdropping on confidential *communications,*" prohibited the unconsented recording of *conversations* between a person in police custody and his or her attorney, religious advisor, or physician, indicating the terms were at the time considered equivalent. (Stats.1957, ch.

Intent

1879, § 1, p. 3285; see Van Boven, *Electronic Surveillance in California: A Study in State Legislative Control* (1969) 57 Cal.L.Rev. 1182, 1191, fn. 48 ["Section 653i proscribed the ... recording of privileged *communications*" (emphasis added)].) Section 653j changed the wording to "communication," but, in view of the equivalency the Legislature accorded to the terms, this does not indicate any substantial increase in the breadth of the criminal prohibition, certainly not such an increase as would sweep along with it sexual conduct. More likely is the intent to include writings that were visually recorded.

The majority mentions the difference between the use of the term "communication" in section 632 and the use of "oral communication" in 18 U.S.C. §§ 2510–2511. However, there is nothing in the California legislative history that indicates the more limited language of the federal statute was considered in drafting section 632, and, more on point, there is no indication whatever that the distinction indicated a legislative intent to include sexual conduct as a kind of communication. (See Van Boven, *supra*, 57 Cal.L.Rev. at p. 1210 ["the 'oral' communications protected in the federal statute are substantially the same as the 'confidential' communications of section 632"].)

Section 630 sets forth the legislative intent in passing Assembly Bill 860, but cannot be read to support the majority's construction. That section makes clear that the purpose of the act was *not* to prevent all invasions of privacy, but only those invasions resulting from "the development of new devices and techniques for the purpose of eavesdropping upon private communications…" Thus, it makes clear that the Legislature was interested in protecting privacy by forbidding recording of private communications as a kind of "time-delayed" eavesdropping. The gravamen of recording private sexual conduct is not time-delayed eavesdropping, but time-delayed voyeurism, a wrong more directly related to section 647, subdivision (h), the "Peeping Tom" loitering subdivision. While voyeurism is clearly an invasion of privacy, section 630 nowhere indicates the Legislature's intention to protect privacy by punishing voyeurism. To construe Assembly Bill 860 as an anti-voyeurism statute is the kind of judicial legislation condemned in *Keeler*.

> Intent

> Precedent

Furthermore, the legislative history of AB 860 is replete with references to conversations, not nonverbal acts, as the equivalent of communications. The "Digest of Assembly Bill 860 (As Amended, June 5, 1967)" by then Assembly Speaker Jesse M. Unruh notes that "Under existing law, Penal Code section 653j, confidential *conversations* may be eavesdropped upon or recorded if only one party to the *conversation* gives his consent." (P. 3.) This at once shows the Assembly Speaker, and sole sponsor of Assembly Bill 860, equated the "communication" sections 653j and 632 with conversation, and shows the defect in section 653j that primarily motivated the adoption of section 632—that a participant could consent to the eavesdropping or recording of a communication without the consent of all participants.

> Intent

The understanding of the term "communication" as referring to a conversation is also evidenced by a memorandum in the State

Archives file on Assembly Bill 860 to Speaker Unruh's legislative assistant from "Clyde Blackmon, Consultant, Committee on Criminal Procedure." It states with reference to section 653j, "The premise underlying the law is that recording a *conversation* or authorizing an outsider to eavesdrop is permissible...." (P. 3.) How the Legislature viewed the term "communication" in section 653j indicates how the Legislature understood the same term in section 632 because the "Bill Digest" prepared for the public hearing on April 25, 1967, before the Assembly Committee on Criminal Procedure states that section 632, subdivision (c), "Defines the words 'confidential communication' and is adapted without change from the existing section 653j(c)." (P. 2.)

Intent

Thus, the legislative history shows that the Legislature never considered the issue of recording private activities as opposed to conversations, much less sexual conduct, and was intent upon protecting privacy by preventing the recording of verbal communication. Without any support in the legislative history, the majority's unusual construction of communication to include sexual conduct is without support and a violation of the separation of powers prohibition against judicial legislation as well as the due process requirement that a defendant have fair notice that a statute applies to the act he or she committed.

I now reach the third aid to proper construction of a statute, case law, and find that as unsupportive of the majority's interpretation of the term "communication" as is the language and legislative history of section 632.

The majority quotes the California Supreme Court to the effect that almost any act could be an attorney-client communication if it were intended as such. (*City & County of S.F. v. Superior Court*) We first observe that the act specifically considered in that case was "a neurological and psychiatric examination" requested by the client's attorneys. The Supreme Court held that the examination and its results came within the attorney-client privilege, the doctor being "an intermediate agent for communication" likening the examination to the examples listed in the full quotation of the above passage taken from 8 Wigmore, Evidence, (3d Ed.1940): " 'The client,

Precedent

supposedly, may make a specimen of his handwriting for the attorney's information, or may exhibit an identifying scar, or may show a secret token. If any of these acts are done as part of a communication to the attorney, and if further the communication is intended to be confidential…, the privilege comes into play.'"

I have no quarrel with the Supreme Court's holding, but find it inapplicable. Conceivably an attorney might engage an expert to evaluate an injured plaintiff's sexual performance in the context of trying to prove injury, in which case any sexual conduct evaluated would come within the privilege as part of a communication to the attorney. However, in that context the sexual conduct per se would not be the communication with the attorney any more than would be any message in the words written as a sample of a client's handwriting. It is the characteristics of the act, not the act itself, that truly constitutes the communication to the lawyer, taking the place of the client's verbal description of the act or condition. Thus, the Supreme Court's holding that an act may be a communication for the purposes of the attorney-client privilege is not a holding that sexual conduct is communication for the purposes of section 632.

Precedent

Furthermore, even if the rule in attorney-client privilege cases were applicable, a requirement of that rule was not the subject of any evidence or argument in the record I have seen. That requirement is proof that the sexual conduct was intended as a communication instead of merely a pleasurable experience.

The majority opinion cites *Granite Construction Co. v. Superior Court* for the proposition that the construction of a statute so as to punish a particular act for the first time does not violate due process. I do not dissent for that reason; I dissent because there is no language, case, or statute, such as there was in *Granite Construction,* that gave fair notice of the extension of the term "communication" to sexual conduct. [corporation could be prosecuted for manslaughter since § 192 requires only "killing of a human being" as opposed to requirement in other states' statutes of killing "'of a human being… by another'" and §7 defines "person" to include corporation].

The majority misconstrues *People v. Sobiek* to support its argument that "we are convinced defendant received fair warning. There

Tradition

can be little doubt defendant knew that in recording the sexual activity without the woman's consent, he was violating her right of privacy and that 'common social duty' would suggest a 'more circumspect conduct.'" While the court in *Sobiek* does quote a previous case to that effect, the court in the following paragraph narrowly construes the broad statement of law quoted and underlined by the majority: "'common social duty' would have forewarned respondent that 'circumspect conduct' prohibited *robbing* his part-

Precedent

ners and also told him that he was *stealing* 'property of another.'"

Just as section 487, the section Sobiek violated, protects property by punishing the taking of property by theft but does not punish the taking of property by burglary, section 632 protects privacy by punishing the recording of confidential communications but does not punish the recording of private sexual conduct. While "'common social duty' would have forewarned" Sobiek that he was committing theft by stealing his partners' property, "'com-

Tradition

mon social duty' would [*not*] have forewarned" Gibbons that that he was recording a confidential communication by recording private sexual conduct. The forewarning must be of the offense punishable by the statute allegedly violated, not the violation of the

Precedent

broad societal interest that the statute protects.

I conclude that no case law supports the majority's construction of the term "communication" in section 632 to include sexual con-

Text, Intent

duct. Since this construction also subverts the common, ordinary meaning of the term in favor of an unusual meaning finding no support in the legislative history , I find it to be judicial legislation enlarging the scope of section 632 without the fair notice to the defendant required by due process.

The majority and dissenting opinions in *Gibbons* sharply disagree over the meaning of the term "confidential communication," and invoke an array of textual arguments designed to interpret the term, including plain meaning arguments, intratextual arguments, and the use of canons of construction. The intent of the legislature is also proven in a number of ways: by reference to the preamble of the Act, quotations from the sponsor of the bill, comparisons to previous versions of the law and a federal statute, and citation to law review commentary. Both the majority and the dissent cited a number of cases thought to control or inform the decision. The majority opinion also relies on "common social duty," which reflects the majority's desire to enforce traditional norms of decency. Finally, the principal focus of the judges' intent arguments was to establish the policy goals of the statute, and to interpret the law in a manner consistent with those goals.

One of the striking things we discover from this exercise is how often legal arguments incorporate more than one type of legal argument. At one point above, for example, the court quotes precedent that quotes text setting forth the intent of the law. Justice Brandeis made a similar argument to interpret the First Amendment in *Whitney v. California*[187] when he ascribed the following policy choice to the Framers: "Those who won our independence believed that the final end of the state was to make men free to develop their faculties...."[188] When we cite this portion of Brandeis' opinion, we invoke precedent stating that the framers' intent was to make a policy choice in favor of freedom.

Why bother to identify each type of argument asserted by the majority and dissenting judges? It is because the identification of the different types of legal arguments is the first step in the process of legal analysis. Each type of argument has a different structure and draws on different types of evidence of what the law is. The evidence that may be assembled to support an argument and the type of attack that can be mounted against it depends on the structure of the argument. Law students, attorneys, and judges who wish to create, attack, and evaluate legal arguments must first acquire the ability to recognize legal arguments. The next chapter discusses how to create persuasive legal arguments, and subsequent chapters describe how to attack and evaluate each type of legal argument.

---

187. 274 U.S. 375 (1927).
188. *Id.*

CHAPTER 9

Creating Persuasive Arguments

What lawyers sell is the art of advocacy, and their stock in trade consists of legal arguments. In hard cases, where the law is not self-evident, attorneys create arguments to explain the law to clients, to negotiate with other attorneys, and to persuade the courts. The Model Rules of Professional Conduct reminds us that "A lawyer should act with zeal in advocacy upon the client's behalf,"[189] and that attorneys may make "a good faith argument for an extension, modification, or reversal of existing law."[190] Arguing for favorable interpretations of the law is not only a professional service, it is an ethical obligation.

Judges, like attorneys, are also required to create legal arguments that seek to persuade. Not only must they evaluate the strengths and weaknesses of competing arguments, they must explain their rulings in a manner that will be accepted by the parties, by higher courts, and by society as a whole.[191] Persuasive legal ar-

---

189. Model Rules of Professional Conduct, Rule 1.3, Comment [1].

190. *Id.*, Rule 3.1. The lawyer's zeal, however, must be tempered by the obligation not to "knowingly fail to disclose to the tribunal legal authority in the controlling jurisdiction known to the lawyer to be directly adverse to the position of the client and not disclosed by opposing counsel...." *Id.*, Rule 3.3(a)(3).

191. A number of legal scholars have commented on the obligation of judges to explain their decisions. H.L.A. Hart identified three "judicial virtues" that are the hallmark of an "acceptable" judicial opinion:

impartiality and neutrality in surveying the alternatives; consideration for the interest of all who will be affected; and a concern to deploy some acceptable general principle as a reasoned gument is as much an obligation of the judge as it is of the practitioner.[192]

How does an attorney or a judge construct a persuasive brief or legal opinion? It is common to think of legal reasoning as consisting of a "chain" of arguments, logically connected one to the other, culminating in a definitive interpretation of the law. But there is a more accurate metaphor. Rather than conceiving of legal argumentation as a "chain," persuasive legal argumentation is more accurately described as a "cable." Professors Eskridge and Frickey draw this contrast between a cable and a chain:

> A chain is no stronger than its weakest link, because if any of the singly connected links should break, so too will the chain. In contrast, a cable's strength relies not on that of individual threads, but upon their cumula-

---

basis for decision. No doubt because a plurality of such principles is always possible it cannot be demonstrated that a decision is uniquely correct: but it may be made acceptable as the reasoned product of informed impartial choice.

HART, THE CONCEPT OF LAW, *supra* note 20, at 205.

M.B.W. Sinclair agrees that purely intuitive reasons are not acceptable as judicial reasoning:

Although, "I decide thus-and-so because: this is how I was brought up; my horizons dictate so; my education, religion, and socialization force me to it; my breakfast didn't agree with me" may describe judicial motivation in some cases, they are not acceptable as justifications in opinions.

M.B.W. Sinclair, *Statutory Reasoning*, 46 DRAKE L. REV. 299, 331 (1997).

Benjamin Cardozo explained how society's acceptance of judicial decisions depends upon the judgment of lawyers: "Only experts may be able to gauge the quality of [the judge's] work and appraise its significance. But their judgment, the judgment of the lawyer class, will spread to others, and tinge the common consciousness and the common faith." CARDOZO, THE NATURE OF THE JUDICIAL PROCESS, *supra* note 1, at 35.

192. The obligation to produce judicial opinions "expos[es] judicial decisions to the discipline of reason and judicial reasoning to the judgment of the world." Robert W. Bennett, *Objectivity in Constitutional Law*, 132 U. PA. L. REV. 445, 479 (1984).

tive strength as they are woven together. Legal arguments are often constructed as chains, but they tend to be more successful when they are cable-like.[193]

What makes a legal argument resemble a cable rather than a chain? A legal argument that is a cable is one that weaves together the different types of legal argument. A brief or a judicial opinion that cites text, intent, precedent, tradition, and policy, all tending toward a single interpretation of the law, is far more persuasive than one that utilizes a single type of argument. When every method of legal argument points to the same conclusion, it creates an impression of inevitability.

Chief Justice John Marshall achieved this effect in *Marbury v. Madison* by weaving a cable of arguments. One of the core holdings of the Court in *Marbury* is that the courts are both authorized and obligated to strike down laws that conflict with the Constitution, and Marshall invoked a variety of arguments to support that conclusion. First, Marshall made a number of intratextual arguments. From the general jurisdiction clause of Article III extending the power of the federal courts to "all cases arising under the constitution,"[194] Marshall concluded that the federal courts must give effect to the constitution.[195] From specific provisions prohibiting state taxes on exports,[196] ex post facto laws,[197] and convictions for treason based on the testimony of a single witness,[198] Marshall inferred that "the framers of the constitution contemplated that instrument as a rule for the government of courts, as well as of the legislature."[199] After observing that the constitution requires judges

---

193. Eskridge & Frickey, *Practical Reasoning, supra* note 2, at 351.

194. "The judicial power of the United States is extended to all cases arising under the constitution." Art. III, sec. 2, cl. 1.

195. "Could it be the intention of those who gave this power, to say that in using it the constitution should not be looked into?" 5 U.S. 137, 179.

196. Art. I, sec. 9, cl. 5.

197. Art. I, sec. 9, cl. 3.

198. Art. III, sec. 3, cl. 1.

199. 5 U.S. 137, 179–180.

to take an oath to support the constitution,[200] he concluded that it would be immoral if the constitution did not permit judges to enforce it.[201] Finally, he inferred the superiority of the constitution to mere statutes from the phrasing of the Supremacy Clause.[202]

In addition to these textual arguments Marshall proffered powerful policy and tradition arguments in support of the principle of judicial review. He observed that if statutes that are contrary to the constitution are binding law, "then written constitutions are absurd attempts, on the part of the people, to limit a power in its own nature illimitable." He added:

> This doctrine would subvert the very foundation of all written constitutions.... That it thus reduces to nothing what we have deemed the greatest improvement on political institutions, a written constitution, would of itself be sufficient, in America, where written constitutions have been viewed with so much reverence, for rejecting the construction.[203]

By interweaving textual, intent, tradition, and policy arguments, all pointing to the same conclusion, Marshall makes the court's decision in Marbury seem inevitable. By drawing together these separate strands Marshall created a powerful legal argument in support

---

200. "The Senators and Representatives before mentioned, and the Members of the several State Legislatures, and all executive and judicial Officers, both of the United States and of the several States, shall be bound by Oath or Affirmation to support this Constitution...." Art. VI, cl. 3.

201. "Why otherwise does it direct the judges to take an oath to support it? This oath certainly applies in an especial manner, to their conduct in their official character. How immoral to impose it on them, if they were to be used as the instruments, and the knowing instruments, for violating what they swear to support!" 5 U.S. 137, 180.

202. "It is also not entirely unworthy of observation, that in declaring what shall be supreme law of the land, the constitution is first mentioned; and not the laws of the United States generally, but those only which shall be made in pursuance of the constitution, have that rank." *Id.*

203. *Id.* at 178.

of the principle of judicial review.[204] Marshall makes Marbury seem
like an easy case.

Accordingly, the first rule to follow in creating persuasive legal
arguments is to invoke more than one type of legal argument.[205]
Do not rest upon a single argument, such as a textual interpretation or the citation of a single case. It is more persuasive to weave
together all of the different types of legal argument in support of
an interpretation of the law.[206] When the text of a legal rule, the in-

---

204. In describing Marshall's opinion in Marbury, Akhil Amar notes:
Missing from this mosaic, interestingly, is precedent. Although
Marshall could have invoked various judicial decisions in support
of his analysis of judicial review—prior state court invocations
of state constitutions against state legislatures, a famous circuit
court ruling striking down a federal statute, an earlier Supreme
Court case invalidating a state statute on Supremacy Clause
grounds—he does not.
Akhil Amar, *Foreward: The Document and the Doctrine*, 114 HARV. L. REV.
26, 32 (2000).
205. "[T]he most satisfying opinions deploy a multiplicity of modes."
Bobbitt, *Reflections, supra* note 22, at 1937. "Whether ultimately correct,
the opinion in Griffin, by its strategy of cumulative assessment and weighing of factors potentially relevant to interpretation, seems more persuasive than would any foundationalist avenue to the same result." Eskridge
and Frickey, *Practical Reasoning, supra* note 2, at 349.
206. For example, Professor Paul Wangerin suggests that law students
should follow this "recipe" for learning to write legal arguments:
    I. Introduction
    II. Facts
    III. Applicable Statutes Support the Stated Answer
    IV. A Large Body of Case Law Also Supports the Stated An-
    swer
    V. The Decision in a Factually Similar Case Lends Additional
    Support
    VI. A Consistent Underlying Policy Is Reflected in All of the
    Cases and Statutes Previously Discussed
    VII. Finally, This Underlying Policy Shows That Apparently
    Contradictory Cases Support the Stated Answer
    VIII. Conclusion

tent of its drafters, judicial precedent, relevant tradition, and policy analysis all militate in favor of a single interpretation of the law, the reasoning seems airtight. Where all five types of legal argument yield the same answer, it would appear to be an easy case. In writing a brief or preparing for oral argument, effective advocates attempt to incorporate all five kinds of legal argument into their presentation. Each of the arguments serves different values—objectivity, popular sovereignty, consistency, societal coherence, and sensitivity to consequences—and each deserves to be considered.

Second, one should carefully consider the order in which the arguments are presented. The list of the types of legal arguments from text to policy analysis presents a natural progression from objective statements of what the law is to subjective judgments as to its proper interpretation. Text is relatively definite evidence of what the law is, while policy arguments are relatively subjective. However, in any particular case one might decide to lead with another type of argument. For example, it may be that in one case precedent is determinative of the outcome, or that in another the intent of the drafters is both incontrovertible and conclusive.

Third, it is critical to keep in mind that law is not a science. Legal reasoning is not deductive, but rhetorical.[207] The goal of legal argument is not to describe a true state of affairs, but to persuade others to adopt your view of what the law is.[208] Legal argument is not an act of discovery, but is rather a demonstration or a dramatic production. Drama is based on conflict, and a persuasive legal argu-

---

Paul T. Wangerin, *Skills Training in "Legal Analysis": A Systematic Approach*, 40 U. MIAMI L. REV. 409, 473 (1986).

207. See Linda Levine & Kurt Saunders, *Thinking Like a Rhetor*, 43 J. LEGAL EDUC. 108 (1993) (suggesting that legal education should incorporate training in classical rhetorical techniques).

208. "[L]egal reasoning entails a practice of argumentation. The reasons given for the conclusions reached are to be measured by their persuasiveness, not by reference to some established true state of affairs." Donald H.J. Hermann, *Legal Reasoning as Argumentation*, 12 N. KY. L. REV. 467, 507 (1985).

ment both acknowledges the conflict and presents your side of the conflict to the listener in a compelling way. The goal of legal argument is to persuade the listener, whether it is a client, another attorney, or a court, to resolve the conflict in the manner you suggest.

Finally, you must scrutinize all of the legal arguments for weak points. Your opponent's arguments must be examined to determine how they can be attacked, and your own arguments must be examined so that you can anticipate your opponent's attacks. In hard cases the legal arguments are susceptible to both "intra-type" and "cross-type" attacks, which are described in the following chapters.

CHAPTER 10

How to Attack Legal Arguments

There are two basic approaches to attacking legal arguments: there are *intra-type* and *cross-type* attacks.[209]

Because each type of legal argument has a different structure and is based upon different evidence of what the law is, each type of argument has characteristic strengths and weaknesses, and may be attacked in characteristic ways. An attack upon a constituent element of a legal argument, or the assertion of another argument of the same type, is an *intra-type* attack.

In contrast, *cross-type* attacks are comparisons between different types of legal arguments. A cross-type attack asserts that the opponent's legal argument is overcome by a competing legal argument of a different type.

The difference between an intra-type and a cross-type attack is illustrated by the following example. Suppose that one attorney has asserted a legal argument based upon precedent. An opposing attorney could mount an *intra-type* attack by challenging the authoritativeness or applicability of the cited case. In addition, the opposing attorney could mount a *cross-type* attack by asserting that the weight of the precedent is subordinated to a competing policy.

It is vital for an attorney to be familiar with both intra-type and cross-type attacks because the persuasiveness of a legal argument

---

209. The terms "intra-type" and "cross-type," suggested by Elizabeth Reilly, correspond to the terms "intramodal" and "cross-modal" proposed by Professors Balkin and Levinson. J.M. Balkin & Sanford Levinson, *Constitutional Grammar*, 72 Tex. L. Rev. 1771, 1796 (1994).

depends on its ability to withstand both kinds of attacks. There are 26 intra-type attacks and two cross-type attacks listed below.

INTRA-TYPE ATTACKS

I. ATTACKS ON TEXTUAL ARGUMENTS
   A. ATTACKS ON ARGUMENTS BASED UPON PLAIN MEANING
      1. The Text Is Ambiguous
      2. The Text Has a Different Plain Meaning
   B. ATTACKS ON THE CANONS OF CONSTRUCTION
      3. The Canon of Construction Does Not Apply
      4. A Conflicting Canon of Construction Applies
   C. ATTACKS ON INTRATEXTUAL ARGUMENTS
      5. There is a Conflicting Intratextual Inference Drawn From the Same Text
      6. There is a Conflicting Intratextual Inference Drawn From Different Text

II. ATTACKS ON INTENT ARGUMENTS
      7. The Intent Was Different
      8. The Evidence of Intent Is Not Sufficient
      9. The Framers of the Law Did Not Anticipate Current Events
      10. The Person Whose Intent Was Proven Did Not Count

III. ATTACKS ON PRECEDENT ARGUMENTS
      11. The Court's Opinion Was Not Holding But Rather Obiter Dictum
      12. The Opinion Did Not Command a Majority of the Court
      13. The Opinion Was Not Issued By a Controlling Authority
      14. The Case Is Distinguishable Because of Dissimilar Facts
      15. The Case is Distinguishable For Policy Reasons
      16. There Are Two Conflicting Lines of Authority
      17. The Case Has Been Overruled
      18. The Case Should Be Overruled

IV. ATTACKS ON TRADITION ARGUMENTS
      19. No Such Tradition Exists
      20. There Have Been Competing Traditions

Chapters 11 through 15 discuss the 26 intra-type attacks on legal arguments, and Chapters 16 through 22 cover the two kinds of cross-type attacks.

Chapter 11

Intra-Type Attacks on Textual Arguments

When a lawyer argues that the language of the law means one thing, an opposing lawyer is likely to respond that the authors of the law meant something else. This typical response to a textual argument sets up a conflict between text and intent, and because it involves a conflict between two different types of arguments, it is an example of a *cross-type* argument that will be discussed in Chapters 16 to 22. In contrast, in this chapter and the four that follow I describe the most common *intra-type* attacks. These are arguments that either challenge one of the constituent elements of a legal argument, or that respond to an argument of one type with another argument of the same type.

A. Intra-Type Attacks on Plain Meaning Arguments

There are two ways to attack an argument that interprets the law based upon the plain meaning of the text: first, one may argue that the text is ambiguous; second, one may argue that the text has a different plain meaning.

1. The Text Is Ambiguous

The most common intra-type attack on a plain meaning argument is to assert that the meaning of the text under consideration is not in fact "plain," but rather that the text is ambiguous. In

McCulloch v. Maryland,[210] the State of Maryland argued that the word "necessary" in the Necessary and Proper Clause meant "indispensable,"[211] and that therefore the Congress had authority to adopt only those measures that were indispensable to carrying out their duties. Justice Marshall responded by observing that human language is inherently ambiguous, and he identified the ambiguity inherent to the word "necessary:"

> Is it true, that this is the sense in which the word necessary is always used? ... Such is the character of human language, that no word conveys to the mind, in all situations, one single definite idea. ... [The word necessary] has not a fixed character peculiar to itself. It admits of all degrees of comparison. ... A thing may be necessary, very necessary, or indispensably necessary.[212]

The distinction between "plain" and "ambiguous" statutory text is critical in any case where there is a presumption about the meaning of legal text, because these presumptions apply only if the text is ambiguous. As one federal court said, "[A] rule of construction is apposite only when Congress has blown an uncertain trumpet. ..."[213] For example, the "rule of lenity" requiring the strict construction of criminal statutes only applies if the statute is ambiguous.[214] Similarly, an administrative agency's construction of a statute is presumptively valid only in cases where the statute is

---

210. 17 U.S. 316 (1819).

211. *Id.* at 413.

212. *Id.*

213. Passamaquoddy Tribe v. Maine, 75 F.3d 784, 793 (1st Cir. 1996).

214. Smith v. United States, 508 U.S. 223 (1993). "The mere possibility of articulating a narrower construction, however, does not by itself make the rule of lenity applicable. Instead, that venerable rule is reserved for cases where, "[a]fter 'seiz[ing] every thing from which aid can be derived'" the Court is 'left with an ambiguous statute.'" *Id.* at 239.

ambiguous. This presumption, known as the *Chevron* doctrine,[215] is one of the core principles of administrative law. If a court finds that the meaning of a statute is unambiguous, then the administrative agency must follow the interpretation laid down by the court. In a series of administrative law cases, the justices of the Supreme Court have disagreed about whether or not the meaning of statutory terms such as "modify" or "stationary source" is plain or ambiguous, and accordingly they disagree about whether or not the agency's interpretation of those terms is presumptively valid.[216]

Another case illustrating the importance of the distinction between "plain" and "ambiguous" statutory language arose under the Freedom of Information Act (FOIA). Under the FOIA, if the government wants to withhold information that a citizen has requested, the government has the burden of proving that the information is covered by an exemption to the law. In *John Doe Agency v. John Doe Corp,*[217] the issue was whether records which had been originally assembled for other purposes and later included as part of a criminal investigation report were "compiled for law enforcement purposes" within the meaning of an exemption to the FOIA and therefore not discoverable. Exemptions to the FOIA are supposed to be "narrowly construed" in order to promote openness in government. In interpreting this provision of the statute, however, the majority found that

---

215. The doctrine was announced in Chevron, U.S.A., Inc. v. Natural Resources Defense Council, Inc., 467 U.S. 837, *reh. den.* 468 U.S. 1227 (1984).

216. *Chevron* interpreted the term "major stationary source" from the Clean Air Act. The issue was whether the Environmental Protection Agency had the authority to redefine major stationary sources using the plantwide "bubble concept," or whether it was required to consider each emitting device as a separate stationary source. In M.C.I. Telecommunications Corp v. American Telephone and Telegraph Co., 512 U.S. 218 (1994), the Court considered whether the F.C.C. had the authority to authorize a long distance carrier to not file a rate tariff, pursuant to its authority under the Federal Communications Act to "modify any requirement" under the Act. The *M.C.I.* case is discussed in detail in Chapter 3.

217. 493 U.S. 146 (1989).

the exemption was not ambiguous. The majority held: "The plain words contain no requirement that compilation be effected at a specific time."[218] Accordingly, the Court denied the request for production of the documents. In contrast, Justice Scalia in dissent concluded that the preferable meaning of the term "compiled" is "originally compiled" and that the records in question were therefore not "compiled for law enforcement purposes." He added that because the exemption was at least ambiguous, it should therefore be interpreted narrowly. Justice Scalia stated: "But even if the meaning of 'compiled' I suggest is not necessarily the preferable one, it is unquestionably a reasonable one; and that creates an ambiguity; and our doctrine of 'narrowly construing' FOIA exemptions requires that ambiguity to be resolved in favor of defendants."[219]

Thus, if the meaning of legal text is unambiguous, the text will be interpreted according to its plain meaning. On the other hand, if legal text is susceptible to more than one meaning, it may be interpreted according to a presumption created by a canon of construction or by substantive law.

2. The Text Has a Different Plain Meaning

The second type of intra-type response to a plain meaning argument is to contend that the plain meaning of the text is different from what is asserted by the opponent. For example, in *Smith v. United States*,[220] the defendant had bartered a gun in exchange for narcotics, and was charged with violating a federal statute that made it unlawful to "use" a firearm during the commission of a drug trafficking offense.[221] The majority held that the statute unambiguously applied to the facts of the case and affirmed the de-

---

218. *Id.* at 153.
219. *Id.* at 164.
220. 508 U.S. 223 (1993).
221. 18 U.S.C. 924(c)(1).

fendant's conviction.[222] In contrast, the dissent concluded that the "ordinary meaning" of the statutory language required that the firearm be used "as a weapon."[223]

B. Intra-Type Attacks on the Canons of Construction

The two kinds of intra-type attacks against arguments based upon canons of construction are either that the canon does not apply to the case under consideration, or that there is a competing canon that applies.

3. The Canon of Construction Does Not Apply

As noted above, one situation where canons of construction are inapplicable is where the meaning of the text is plain. Thus, a common way to attack the applicability of a canon of construction is to assert that the text is unambiguous. In *United States v. Krizek*,[224] for example, the D.C. Circuit Court of Appeals stated that "the rule of lenity is invoked only when the statutory language is ambiguous."[225] But there are other ways to attack the applicability of a canon of construction. The rule of lenity only applies to penal statutes, and is accordingly not usually invoked in civil cases.[226] Another canon, "remedial statutes are to be liberally construed," does not apply unless the statute in question is remedial. In objecting to the use of this canon of construction, Justice Scalia remarked that "there is not

---

222. 508 U.S. 223, 239. Because it found the statute to be unambiguous, the majority declined to apply the "rule of lenity." *Id.*
223. *Id.* at 242. Eric Lasky identified the *Smith* case as containing an example of competing "plain meaning" interpretations in *Perplexing Problems with Plain Meaning*, 27 Hofstra L. Rev. 891 (1999).
224. 111 F.3d 934 (D.C.Cir. 1997).
225. *Id.* at 942.
226. *Id.*

the slightest agreement on what its subject—the phrase 'remedial statutes'—consists of."[227]

4. A Conflicting Canon of Construction Applies

The legal realists regarded the textual methods of interpretation with skepticism. In particular, they believed that the canons of construction could be manipulated to generate a variety of different textual interpretations. Karl Llewellyn, a leading realist, assembled a list of fifty-six canons of statutory construction, and suggested that for each and every canon of construction there is an equal and opposite canon.[228] For example, the substantive canon "remedial statutes are to be liberally construed," conflicts with another substantive canon, "statutes in derogation of the common law are to be strictly construed." In what must be a typical situation, how are we to interpret a remedial statute that alters the common law? Another example of "competing canons" is the conflict between *expressio unius est exclusio alterius* (the negative implication) and *ejusdem generis* (extension by analogy to similar cases). This conflict is easy to illustrate. Suppose that there is a sign outside a restaurant that says, "Dogs Allowed." May I bring in my cat? The canon *expressio unius* would suggest that the mention of dogs implicitly negates the inclusion of cats, while a variant of the canon *ejusdem generis* suggests cats *are* allowed because the rule should be extended to other housepets. Contemporary legal scholars differ on the question of whether the canons of construction are useful guides for decisionmaking or whether, as Llewellyn implied, they are simply conclusory.[229]

---

227. Scalia, *Canards, supra* note 51, at 583.

228. Karl Llewellyn, *Remarks on the Theory of Appellate Decision and the Rules or Canons About How Statutes Are to Be Construed*, 3 VAND. L. REV. 395, 401 (1950).

229. Edward Rubin agrees with Llewellyn, and states that in the modern administrative state, where statutes are "a mechanism for allocating resources and deploying force," the canons of construction are "increasingly irrelevant." Edward L. Rubin, *Modern Statutes, Loose Canons, and the Lim-*

C. Intra-Type Attacks on Intratextual Arguments

Intra-type attacks on intratextual arguments also take two forms. One may argue that there is a conflicting inference that may be drawn from the same text, or that there is a conflicting inference that may be drawn from other text in the same document.

5. There Is a Conflicting Intratextual Inference Drawn from the Same Text

In *Barron v. Baltimore*,[230] the Supreme Court was called upon to decide whether the Just Compensation Clause of the Fifth Amendment was applicable against the States. The language of the Fifth Amendment appears to be universal, declaring "nor shall private property be taken for public use, without just compensation." It does not state whether it is binding on the federal government, on the states, or on both. In *Barron* the Supreme Court noted that Art. I, sec. 10 of the original Constitution expressly stated that "No state shall" enter into treaties, coin money, or pass any ex post facto laws. From this the Court concluded that, "[Had] the framers of [the] amendments intended them to be limitations on the powers of the state governments, they would have imitated the framers of the

---

its of Practical Reason: A Response to Farber and Ross, 45 VAND. L. REV. 579, 579–580 ((1992).

Kent Greenawalt argues that although the textual canons "are not nearly as opposed to one another as has sometimes been claimed.... reliance on canons is too uneven to provide much assurance about the way particular language will be interpreted if its apparent meaning is unclear." GREENAWALT, 20 QUESTIONS, *supra* note 31, at 211.

Other recent scholarly works on this subject include Richard Posner, *Statutory Interpretation—in the Classroom and in the Courtroom*, 50 U. CHI. L. REV. 800, 805–817 (1983); and Jonathan R. Macey & Geoffrey P. Miller, *The Canons of Statutory Construction and Judicial Preferences*, 45 VAND. L. REV. 647 (1992).

230. 32 U.S. 243 (1833).

original constitution, and have expressed that intention."[231] On the other hand, one could argue that the quoted language of Art. I, sec. 10 is evidence that the Constitution of the United States was binding upon the States as well as the federal government, and that therefore in the absence of limiting language the provisions of the Fifth Amendment were equally binding upon the states.

6. There Is a Conflicting Intratextual Inference Drawn from Different Text

As discussed in the previous paragraph, in *Barron v. Baltimore* Justice Marshall drew an inference from the language of Art. I, sec. 10 of the Constitution that the Fifth Amendment was applicable solely against the federal government, and not against the states. However, the noted contemporary scholar William Rawle drew the opposite inference from different language in the Constitution. In his 1829 treatise on the Constitution, Rawle pointed to the language of the First Amendment, which states: "Congress shall make no law respecting an establishment of religion, or prohibiting the free exercise thereof; or abridging the freedom of speech, or of the press...." Rawle observed that, in contrast to the First Amendment, the remaining provisions of the Bill of Rights are not by their terms limited to Congress, and he concluded that the other Amendments are alike applicable to the States as to the national government:

> The preceding article [the First Amendment] expressly refers to the powers of congress alone, but some of those which follow are to be more generally construed, and considered as applying to the state legislatures as well as that of the Union. The important principles contained in them are now incorporated by adoption into the instrument itself; they form parts of the declared rights of

---

231. *Id.* at 250.

the people, of which neither the state power nor those of the Union can ever deprive them.[232]

In summary, each type of textual argument may be challenged in characteristic ways. One may attack the persuasiveness or applicability of the interpretive textual technique, or invoke a competing textual interpretation.

232. WILLIAM RAWLE, A VIEW OF THE CONSTITUTION OF THE UNITED STATES OF AMERICA 124–125 (1970).

CHAPTER 12

Intra-Type Attacks on
Intent Arguments

Intent arguments interpret the law in accordance with the intent of the people who created the law. There are four common ways of attacking arguments based upon intent. One may seek to prove that the intent of the authors of the legal text was different from what the opponent asserts. One may challenge the nature and the amount of evidence that was presented to prove the drafters' intent. One may argue that the persons who adopted the instrument could not have foreseen current conditions. Or one may challenge the assumption that the person whose intent was proven was a drafter of the law.

7. The Intent Was Different

The most basic way to attack an argument based upon the intent of the persons who drafted a law is to argue that their intent was different from what the opponent asserts. Two of the most significant rebuttals of this type issued from Abraham Lincoln, and both ultimately concerned the issue of slavery.

At the time of the *Dred Scott* case, Chief Justice Roger Taney and Senator Stephen Douglas contended that the signers of the Declaration of Independence did not intend to include blacks when they wrote that "all men are created equal." In his speech of June 26, 1857, at Springfield, Illinois, Abraham Lincoln passionately argued that the signers of the Declaration of Independence *did* intend to include blacks.

> I think the authors of that notable instrument intended to include *all* men, but they did not intend to de-

clare all men equal *in all respects.* They did not mean
to say all were equal in color, size, intellect, moral de-
velopments, or social capacity. They defined with tol-
erable distinctness, in what respects they did consider
all men created equal—equal in "certain inalienable
rights, among which are life, liberty, and the pursuit of
happiness." This they said, and this meant. They did
not mean to assert the obvious untruth, that all were
then actually enjoying that equality, nor yet, that they
were about to confer it immediately upon them. In fact
they had no power to confer such a boon. They meant
simply to declare the *right,* so that the *enforcement* of
it might follow as fast as circumstances should permit.[233]

Another even more "lawyerly" rebuttal to an intent argument by
Taney and Douglas formed the core of Lincoln's speech at Cooper
Union on February 27, 1860. This was the speech which brought
Lincoln to national attention, and the principal argument that Lincoln advanced was that the framers of the Constitution had intended for the federal government to have the power to abolish or
restrict slavery in the federal territories. Lincoln laid the groundwork for his argument by identifying whose intent mattered:

> Who were our fathers that framed the Constitution?
> I suppose the "thirty-nine" who signed the original in-
> strument may be fairly called our fathers who framed
> that part of the present Government. It is almost ex-
> actly true to say they framed it, and it is altogether true
> to say they fairly represented the opinion and sentiment
> of the whole nation at that time.[234]

Lincoln then proceeded to prove that virtually all of these indi-
viduals had either voted for or expressed support for federal legis-

---

233. ABRAHAM LINCOLN, 2 COLLECTED WORKS OF ABRAHAM LINCOLN
405–406 (P. Basler, ed. 1953).
234. 3 COLLECTED WORKS, at 523.

lation controlling slavery on federal land, demonstrating that the intent of the framers on this point was directly contrary to what Chief Justice Taney had found in *Dred Scott*.[235]

8. The Evidence of Intent Is Not Sufficient

In rebutting an argument based upon intent it is not necessary to prove what the intent of the authors was; it is instead sufficient to prove that we cannot be confident what their intent was. The most significant example of this second kind of intra-type attack on an intent argument comes from the landmark case of *Brown v. Board of Education*. In the following passage from that opinion, Chief Justice Earl Warren described how the Court had sought additional guidance from the parties concerning the original intent of the framers of the Fourteenth Amendment with regard to the desegregation of the public schools:

> Reargument was largely devoted to the circumstances surrounding the adoption of the Fourteenth Amendment in 1868. It covered exhaustively consideration of the Amendment in Congress, ratification by the states, then existing practices in racial segregation, and the views of proponents and opponents of the Amendment. This discussion and our own investigation convince us that, although these sources cast some light, it is not enough to resolve the problem with which we are faced. At best, they are inconclusive. The most avid proponents of the post-War Amendments undoubtedly intended them to remove all legal distinctions among "all persons born or naturalized in the United States." Their opponents, just as certainly, were antagonistic to both the letter and the spirit of the Amendments and wished them to have the most limited effect. What others in

---

235. *Id.* at 522–527.

congress and the state legislatures had in mind cannot be determined with any degree of certainty.[236]

In another seminal case, *Youngstown Sheet & Tube v. Sawyer*,[237] Justice Robert Jackson expressed misgivings about the value of the evidence of the framers' intent on the question of the President's emergency power under the Constitution. Jackson said: "Just what our forefathers did envision, or would have envisioned had they foreseen modern conditions, must be divined from materials almost as enigmatic as the dreams Joseph was called upon to interpret for Pharaoh."[238]

The same issue arises in the interpretation of statutes. When one attorney proffers evidence of the intent of the legislature, opposing counsel may attack the strength of the evidence of intent, or offer conflicting evidence, or both. Robert Jackson has pithy advice for us on this subject: "It is a poor cause that cannot find some plausible support in legislative history."[239] There are a number of different types of evidence of legislative intent, and legal scholars have evaluated the relative persuasiveness of each category of evidence. In addition to the list compiled by Mikva and Lane described in Chapter 4, there is the following "Hierarchy of Legislative History" proposed by Professors William Eskridge and Philip Frickey:

1. Committee Reports
2. Sponsor Statements
3. Rejected Proposals
4. Floor and Hearing Colloquy

---

236. 347 U.S. 483, 489 (1954).

237. 343 U.S. 579 (1952).

238. *Id.* at 634.

239. Robert H. Jackson, *Problems of Statutory Interpretation*, 8 F.R.D. 121, 125 (1948). Mikva and Lane responded to Justice Jackson's warning by urging courts to acquire an understanding of the legislative process and to attempt to "choose legislative history that is most probative of legislative intent and not legislative history that supports their views." MIKVA & LANE, *supra* note 85, at 36.

5. Nonlegislative Drafters and Sponsors
6. Legislative Silence and Subsequent History[240]

Attorneys frequently offer competing evidence of what the intent of the framers of a law was.

9. The Framers of the Law Did Not Anticipate Current Conditions

An additional reason expressed by the Supreme Court for not following "the original intent of the framers" in *Brown v. Board of Education* was that their intent was no longer relevant due to changed social conditions. Justice Warren stated:

> An additional reason for the inconclusive nature of the Amendment's history, with respect to segregated schools, is the status of public education at that time. In the South, the movement toward free common schools, supported by general taxation, had not yet taken hold.... Even in the North, the conditions of public education did not approximate those existing today.[241]

The intent of the framers of a law may become less relevant because of changes in society, scientific advances, or new understandings of facts.

10. The Person Whose Intent Was Proven Did Not Count

Whose intent counts? The "Hierarchy of Legislative History" set forth above indicates that, when interpreting statutes, the statements of legislators count more than those of mere citizens, and among legislators, the statements of the sponsors of the legislation are more probative of legislative intent than those of other legislators. Similarly, one legal scholar argues that for purposes of interpreting the

---

240. Eskridge, *The New Textualism*, *supra* note 35, at 636–640.
241. 347 U.S. 483, 489–490.

Constitution, we should not look to the intent of those who met in Constitutional Convention in Philadelphia in 1787, but rather to those who later ratified the Constitution in state conventions.[242]

An intriguing argument regarding "who counts" as a framer of the Constitution involved an attack on the views of Alexander Hamilton. Hamilton richly earned his reputation as an authoritative source on the meaning of the Constitution. Prior to the Revolutionary War, Hamilton authored influential pamphlets supporting the colonists' cause. At the commencement of the war he organized a company of artillery, and based upon his exemplary performance in the field he became General Washington's confidential aide with the rank of Lieutenant-Colonel. He led the attack that overwhelmed the first redoubt at Yorktown. Following the War, at the Annapolis Convention, he was the motive force calling for the Constitutional Convention of 1787. He served at the Constitutional Convention; he authored, with John Jay and James Madison, the Federalist Papers; and through "sheer will and reasoning" he secured the ratification of the Constitution by the New York State convention. Later, as Secretary of the Treasury under George Washington, he issued a succession of opinions on national policy and the organization of the federal government.[243]

Despite Hamilton's courageous and loyal service in gaining our independence and forming our government, Justice William Rehnquist, writing for the majority in *Printz v. United States*,[244] suggested that the views of Alexander Hamilton were not definitive upon the question of the power of the federal government to command the performance of state officials:

---

242. "The framers assuredly gave the document its words; they did not determine the meaning of those words as understood by the ratifiers, by those people whose views were crucial to legitimating the document as fundamental law." Charles A. Lofgren, *The Original Understanding of Original Intent?*, 5 CONS. COMMENT. 77, 84–85 (1988).

243. ENCYCLOPEDIA BRITTANICA 121–122 (1950).

244. 521 U.S. 898 (1997).

Even if we agreed with Justice Souter's reading of the Federalist No. 27 [authored by Hamilton], it would still seem to us most peculiar to give the view expressed in that one piece, not clearly confirmed by any other writer, the determinative weight he does. That would be crediting the most expansive view of federal authority ever expressed, and from the pen of the most expansive expositor of federal power. Hamilton was "from first to last the most nationalistic of all nationalists in his interpretation of the clauses of our federal Constitution."[245]

In summary, arguments based upon the intent of the drafters of a law may be attacked by challenging the nature or sufficiency of the evidence of intent, the adequacy of the framers' knowledge of contemporary conditions, or the qualifications of the person whose intent was proven.

---

245. *Id.* at 915, quoting C. ROSSITER, ALEXANDER HAMILTON AND THE CONSTITUTION 199 (1964).

CHAPTER 13

Intra-Type Attacks on Precedent Arguments

There are eight ways to attack arguments based upon precedent. These include attacks on both the authoritativeness and the applicability of the cited case.

11. The Court's Opinion Was Not Holding but Rather Obiter Dictum

One of the most difficult aspects of analyzing precedent is to determine the precise holding of the court. How much of the court's opinion is essential to the outcome and therefore "holding," and how much of it is merely "dictum?" That was the problem that confronted Chief Justice Warren Burger in *Walz v. Tax Commission.*[246]

The issue in *Walz* was the constitutionality of property tax exemptions for churches. Precedent from earlier cases decided under the Establishment Clause contained broad language forbidding all government assistance to religion. For example, in *Everson v. Board of Education,*[247] the Supreme Court had said: "Neither [a state nor the federal government] can pass laws which aid one religion, aid all religions, or prefer one religion over another."[248] However, despite this broad language, the Court in *Everson* upheld a law under which local school boards repaid parents for the cost of trans-

---

246. 397 U.S. 664 (1970).
247. 330 U.S. 1 (1947).
248. *Id.* at 15.

portation to private and parochial schools. In *Walz*, Justice Burger warned against reliance on "sweeping utterances" contained in prior opinions:

> In attempting to articulate the scope of the two Religion Clauses, the Court's opinions reflect the limitations inherent in formulating general principles on a case-by-case basis. The considerable internal inconsistency in the opinions of the Court derives from what, in retrospect, may have been to[o] sweeping utterances on aspects of these clauses that seemed clear in relation to the particular cases but have limited meaning as general principles.[249]

Another famous example of an objection to a court's opinion because it contained unnecessary reasoning was Thomas Jefferson's attack on Justice Marshall's opinion in *Marbury v. Madison*.[250] In that case William Marbury sued Secretary of State James Madison for a court order (specifically, a writ of mandamus) that would require Madison to deliver to him a commission appointing him as a federal Justice of the Peace. Justice Marshall first determined that Marbury was entitled to the writ of mandamus, but then Marshall held that the Supreme Court lacked jurisdiction to issue the writ. Why didn't Marshall simply dismiss the case for lack of jurisdiction? In a letter to William Johnson dated June 12, 1823, Thomas Jefferson bitterly complained about John Marshall's tendency towards *obiter dictum*:

> This practice of Judge Marshall, of travelling out of his case to prescribe what the law would be in a moot case not before the court, is very irregular and very censurable.... [In *Marbury v. Madison*] [t]he court determined at once, that being an original process, they had

---

249. *Id.* at 668.
250. 5 U.S. 137 (1803).

no cognizance of it; and therefore the question before them was ended. But the Chief Justice went on to lay down what the law would be, had they jurisdiction of the case.... [251]

The principle of *stare decisis*, which provides that the deciding court and all lower courts within the same jurisdiction are bound by the judicial opinion, applies solely to the holding of the court, and not to *obiter dictum*.

12. The Opinion Did Not Command a Majority of the Court

The reasoning contained in dissenting opinions is not binding on future courts for obvious reasons. However, the reasoning of plurality and concurring opinions must be accorded some weight. When the majority of the judges on a multi-member court agree upon a result in a case, even if they disagree as to the proper rationale, the result is binding on future courts. Plurality opinions express the reasoning agreed to by the largest number of judges, and as such are of some precedential value. Where no single line of reasoning commands a majority of the court, the opinion that expresses the narrowest grounds for the result is the reasoning that is binding on future courts.[252]

---

251. BASIC WRITINGS OF THOMAS JEFFERSON 781 (Philip S. Foner, ed. 1944).

252. *See* Marks v. United States, 430 U.S. 188 (1977) (suggesting factors to be considered for determining the holding of the Court in when there is no majority opinion); Triplett Grille v. City of Akron, 40 F.3d 129, 134 (1994), holding that Justice Souter's concurring opinion from Barnes v. Glen Theatre, Inc., 501 U.S. 560 (1991), "resolved the question before the Supreme Court on the narrowest grounds," and thus provided the rule of the case. Another view is that concurring opinions that are necessary to form a majority vote for a result are entitled to added weight. *See* Igor Kirman, *Standing Apart to Be a Part: The Precedential Value of Supreme Court Concurring Opinions*, 95 COLUM. L. REV. 2083 (1995).

Occasionally it may not be clear whether the court's rationale
has been adopted by a majority of the court. In *Hopwood v. Texas*,[253]
the United States Court of Appeals for the Fifth Circuit refused to
follow the opinion of Supreme Court Justice Lewis Powell upholding
"plus factor" affirmative action admissions programs in *Regents of
the University of California v. Bakke*.[254] The Fifth Circuit based its decision in part on this ground: "Justice Powell's opinion in *Bakke*
garnered only his own vote and has never represented the view of
a majority of the Court in *Bakke* or any other case."[255] In *Grutter v.
Bollinger*, however, a majority of the Supreme Court followed *Bakke*
and embraced the reasoning of Justice Powell.[256]

The weight of an opinion cannot be measured solely by the number of votes it garnered when it first was issued. A concurring opinion may gain precedential force if later courts perceive its reasoning
to be more powerful than that of the majority opinion. For example, Justice Robert Jackson's concurrence in *Youngstown Sheet &
Tube v. Sawyer*[257] has at least equaled, if not surpassed, the importance of the majority opinion of Justice Hugo Black.

Factors affecting the precedential weight of dissenting and concurring opinions also include the prestige of the author and whether
the reasoning of the majority opinion has been overruled. For these
reasons, as well as their soaring prose, the dissenting opinion of
the elder Justice Harlan in *Plessy v. Ferguson*,[258] the dissenting opinions of Justice Holmes in *Abrams v. United States*[259] and *Lochner v.*

---

253. 78 F.3d. 932, *cert. den.* 518 U.S. 1033 (1996).
254. 438 U.S. 265, 320 (1978). The policy arguments in Justice Powell's opinion in the *Bakke* case are described in Chapter 15.
255. 78 F.3d 932, 944 (1996).
256. 539 U.S. 306, 323-325 (2003) (O'Connor, J.) (endorsing the reasoning of Justice Powell without resolving the *Marks* issue).
257. 343 U.S. 579 (1952).
258. 163 U.S. 537, 552 (1896). Justice Harlan rejected the majority's
"separate but equal" doctrine upholding segregation of the races.
259. 250 U.S. 616, 624 (1919). In this dissenting opinion Justice Holmes
articulated the bedrock First Amendment principle of "the marketplace
of ideas."

New York,[260] and the concurring opinion of Justice Brandeis in *Whitney v. California*,[261] are today justly considered authoritative. In the First Amendment context, Robert Bork refers to this as "the triumph of Holmes and Brandeis."[262]

13. The Opinion Was Not Issued by a Controlling Authority

Precedential weight depends in part upon the level and jurisdiction of the tribunal rendering the decision. As Judge Leo A. Jackson of the Eighth District Court of Appeals for the State of Ohio once noted: "[We are not] bound by the decisions of our sister Courts of Appeals, although they are entitled to due consideration and respect. We are bound by the decisions of our Supreme Court."[263]

Courts must follow the decisions of higher courts within the same jurisdiction, and apply the doctrine of *stare decisis* to previous decisions of the same court. The precedential weight of decisions by other courts depend upon the location, level, and reputation of the court issuing the decision.

14. The Case Is Distinguishable Because of Dissimilar Facts

One of the most powerful ways to attack an argument based on precedent is to distinguish the prior case. As noted in Chapter 5, to rely on precedent is to reason by analogy. When we follow a previous case, we apply the rule of the previous case by analogy to the case at hand. When we distinguish a previous case, we do not apply

---

260. 198 U.S. 45, 74 (1905). Justice Holmes rejected the "economic substantive due process" reasoning of the majority, and voted to uphold the state's power to adopt maximum hour legislation.

261. 274 U.S. 357, 372 (1927).

262. Bork, *Neutral Principles*, *supra* note 64, at 23.

263. Hogan v. Hogan, 29 Ohio App.2d 69, 77, 278 N.E.2d 367, 372 (1972) (Jackson, J.).

its rule to the case at hand. In logical terms, to apply a case by analogy is to find that there is a *sufficient* condition for applying the rule of the cited case to the case at hand, whereas to distinguish a case is to find that a *necessary* condition for applying the rule of the cited case is lacking.[264]

In easy cases, courts may apply or distinguish prior cases on factual grounds, *i.e.*, because the facts of the cited case are similar or dissimilar to the facts of the case at hand. In most cases it is clear whether or not the facts of the cited case are similar to the facts of the case under consideration. Typical fact patterns emerge in every area of the law, and are efficiently decided by invoking precedent. But in difficult cases, the factual similarity or dissimilarity is not clear. For example, when technological or social change occurs, it becomes difficult to reason by analogy to past cases. The analogies break down because it is not obvious whether the new facts are similar or dissimilar to the facts of the previous cases.

For example, in the 1916 case *McPherson v. Buick Motor Co*,[265] the New York State Court of Appeals was presented with a difficult case at the intersection of the law of tort and contract. Buick Motor Co. had purchased a defective wheel from another manufacturer, assembled the wheel into an automobile, and sold the automobile to a retail dealer, who resold it to a customer. When the wheel broke, the customer was injured. The customer sued Buick on the ground that Buick had negligently failed to inspect the wheel and discover the defect.

This case arose in the context of the widespread and growing carnage on the roads caused by the advent of the automobile. Accordingly, the New York State Court of Appeals was dealing with a novel and serious social problem.

The Court of Appeals considered a number of similar cases where

---

264. Scott Brewer, *Exemplary Reasoning: Semantics, Pragmatics, and the Rational Force of Legal Argument by Analogy*, 109 Harv. L. Rev. 923, 1016 (1996).

265. 217 N.Y. 382 (1916).

people who had been injured by a defective product had sued the manufacturers, even though they had not purchased the product directly from the manufacturer. In those cases the principal stumbling block to the plaintiffs' recovery was that they were not in "privity" with the manufacturer, meaning that they did not have a contractual relationship with the manufacturer. In the past, the general rule was that manufacturers were *not* liable to the ultimate consumers of a product unless the product when sold was "inherently dangerous." Liability had been imposed on remote manufacturers for selling mislabled poisons, defective scaffolding, and coffee urns and bottles of aerated water that exploded. On the other hand, courts had found no liability in cases where the manufacturer had sold a defective circular saw or a defective steam boiler. In the principal case, *Winterbottom v. Wright*,[266] a British court had imposed no liability on the manufacturer of a wagon that had collapsed and injured a passenger. Dissenting in the *McPherson* case, Chief Justice Bartlett cited *Winterbottom*, and drew the following factual analogy:

> In the case at bar the defective wheel on an automobile moving only eight miles an hour was not any more dangerous to the occupants of the car than a similarly defective wheel would be to the occupants of a carriage drawn by a horse at the same speed; and yet unless the courts have been all wrong on this question up to the present time there would be no liability to strangers to the original sale in the case of the horse-drawn carriage.[267]

Justice Bartlett believed that the courts had imposed liability on manufacturers only in cases where "the article sold was of such a character that danger to life or limb was involved in the ordinary use thereof; in other words, where the article sold was inherently dangerous."[268]

---

266. 10 W. & M. 109, 152 Eng. Rep. 402 (Ex. 1842).
267. 217 N.Y. 382, 400 (Bartlett, C.J., dissenting).
268. *Id.* at 396.

Writing for the majority, Justice Cardozo could not persuasively distinguish *Winterbottom* on the facts. Instead, Cardozo turned to a realist analogy, discussed in the following section.

15. The Case Is Distinguishable for Policy Reasons

In *McPherson* one might conclude, like Justice Bartlett, that an automobile is more similar to a wagon than to poison or to scaffolding, and that therefore no liability should be imposed on the defendant Buick Motor Co. But Justice Cardozo declined to rely upon factual analogies. Instead, he drew a realist analogy, observing that "[t]he principle of the distinction is for present purposes the important thing."[269] The Buick Motor Company had argued that liability could be imposed only upon the manufacturers of "poisons, explosives, deadly weapons—things whose normal function it is to injure or destroy."[270] Cardozo noted, however, that the "trend" of the law had been to extend liability to any defective product that was inherently dangerous:

> Whatever the rule ... may once have been, it has no longer that restricted meaning. A large coffee urn may have within itself, if negligently made, the potentcy of danger, yet no one thinks of it as an implement whose normal function is destruction. What is true of the coffee urn is equally true of bottles of aerated water.[271]

Cardozo imposed liability on the Buick Motor Co. on the ground that an automobile "was liable to become a source of great danger to many people if not carefully and properly constructed."[272] He explained that even though *Winterbottom* was factually analogous to *McPherson*, the principle that was at stake in *Winterbottom* would not be served by denying liability, because times had changed:

---

269. *Id.* at 385.
270. *Id.* at 387.
271. *Id.* (citations omitted).
272. *Id.*, quoting Statler v. Ray Mfg. Co., 195 N.Y. 478, 480 (1909).

Precedents drawn from the days of travel by stage coach do not fit the conditions of travel today. The principle that the danger must be imminent does not change, but the things subject to the principle do change. They are whatever the needs of life in a developing civilization require them to be.[273]

In *The Nature of the Judicial Process*, Justice Cardozo disapproved of the practice of drawing analogies to the *facts* of a case as overly simplistic: "Some judges seldom get beyond that process in any case. Their notion of their duty is to match the colors of the case at hand against the colors of many sample cases spread out upon their desk. The sample nearest in shade supplies the applicable rule."[274]

Like Cardozo, other leading legal scholars have criticized the judicial practice of following or distinguishing cases based solely upon factual similarities or dissimilarities. Professor Cass Sunstein has written: "Formalist analogical thinking is no better than any other kind of bad formalism. Different factual situations are inarticulate; they do not impose order on themselves.... Whether one case is analogous to another depends on substantive ideas that must be justified."[275]

For this reason, in difficult cases courts are not satisfied with using "formalist analogies," comparing the similarities and differences in the facts, but are drawn to "realist analogies," in which cases are compared based upon the underlying values that are at stake.

In hard cases it is difficult to determine whether the facts of the cited case are similar to the case to be decided. Are the factual similarities and dissimilarities "important?" Steven Burton refers to this as "the problem of importance."[276] Importance (*i.e.*, similar-

---

273. *Id.* at 391.
274. CARDOZO, THE NATURE OF THE JUDICIAL PROCESS, *supra* note 1, at 20.
275. Sunstein, *supra* note 103, at 756–757.
276. STEVEN BURTON, AN INTRODUCTION TO LAW AND LEGAL REASONING 83 (1985).

ity) is measured by whether the policies underlying the rule from the cited case would be served by applying that rule to the case at hand.[277]

In comparing two contracts cases, for example, Richard Warner argues, "The salient difference between *Columbia* and *Southern Concrete* is that, in the latter, the two companies had never dealt with each other before. Is this a relevant difference? Courts answer such questions by appeal to the legitimate goals and purposes of the law."[278]

H.L.A. Hart makes a similar observation: "In the case of legal rules, the criteria of relevance and closeness of resemblance depend on many complex factors running through the legal system and on the aims or purpose which may be attributed to the rule."[279]

Cass Sunstein warns, however, that realist analogies may be as bad as formalist analogies. In the following passage Sunstein criticizes the realist analogy that Oliver Wendell Holmes used in his shocking decision in *Buck v. Bell*,[280] where the Supreme Court upheld the forced sterilization of people with mental disabilities:

---

277. *See* J.C. Smith, *Machine Intelligence and Legal Reasoning*, 73 CHI.-KENT L. REV. 277, 314–315 (1998).

278. Richard Warner, *Three Theories of Legal Reasoning*, 62 So. CAL. L. REV. 1523, 1539–1540 (1989).

279. HART, THE CONCEPT OF LAW, *supra* note 20, at 127. See M.B.W. Sinclair, *Statutory Reasoning*, *supra* note 191, at 364 ("The criterion of similarity ... comes from the realm of policy....") *See also* Steven M. Quevedo, *Formalist and Instrumentalist Legal Reasoning and Legal Theory*, 73 CAL. L. REV. 119 (1985) (distinguishing between formalist and instrumentalist analogies).

280. 274 U.S. 200 (1927). This case is notorious for many reasons. First, Carrie Buck was in all likelihood not mentally handicapped, merely poor and defenseless. Second, she was quite literally defenseless because there is compelling evidence that her attorney deliberately conspired with her oppressors to uphold the law that subjected her to sterilization. Third, the concluding sentence of Holmes' opinion—"Three generations of imbeciles is enough."—ranks among the cruelest and most unjust utterances in Supreme Court history. *See* Paul A. Lombardo, *Three Generations, No Imbeciles: New Light on Buck v. Bell*, 60 N.Y.U. L. REV. 30 (1985).

Holmes suggested that if people can be conscripted during wartime, or can be forced to obtain vaccinations, it
follows that the state can require sterilization of the 'fee-
ble minded.' But this is a casual and unpersuasive claim.
Many principles may cover the possibly relevant similarities and differences among these cases. He does not
identify the range of possible principles, much less argue
for one rather than another. Instead, he invokes a principle of a high level of generality—"the public welfare may
call upon the best citizens for their lives"—that is not
evaluated by reference to low- or intermediate-level principles that may also account for the analogous cases.[281]

Despite their potential for abuse, realist analogies are a crucial
analytical tool for resolving disputes between competing lines of
authority. This is discussed in the following section.

16. There Are Two Conflicting Lines of Authority

When there are two competing lines of case law—when precedent is conflicting—how is the dispute resolved? In these situations the difference between formalist and realist analysis becomes
apparent. As John Dickinson explained, disputes between competing precedents are resolved realistically, not formalistically:

The choice which a judge makes of one analogy rather
than another is an expression of ... a value-judgment;
and the possibility of competing analogies therefore
arises not merely or so much out of the doubtfulness
of the factual resemblances among his materials, but
rather out of the possibility of differences of opinion as
to the comparative value of the different results which
one analogy or the other would bring about.[282]

---

281. Sunstein, *supra* note 103, at 757.
282. John Dickinson, *The Law Behind Law, supra* note 152, at 290
(1929).

Justice Cardozo agreed with Dickinson that the interpretation of the law turns upon a balancing of the principles or interests that are at stake. Cardozo described how this balancing worked in the case of *Riggs v. Palmer*,[283] in which the court had held that a murderer could not inherit from the person he killed:

> Conflicting principles were there in competition for the mastery. One of them prevailed, and vanquished all the others. There was the principle of the binding force of a will disposing of the estate of a testator [the author of a will] in conformity with law.... There was the principle that civil courts may not add to the pains and penalties of crimes.... But over against these was another principle, of greater generality, its roots deeply fastened in universal sentiments of justice, the principle that no man should profit from his own inequity or take advantage of his own wrong.[284]

When there are competing lines of authority from prior case law, it is important to not simply identify which *facts* of the previous cases are most similar to the case at hand. It is also necessary to identify which *values* or *policies* from previous case law are at stake in the case at hand, and to identify which rule from the prior cases best serves those policies.

17. The Case Has Been Overruled

A judicial decision that has been expressly overruled, of course, has no precedential force, but in some cases it may be unclear whether a prior decision has been overruled in its entirety. The holding of the Supreme Court in *Brown v. Board of Education*,[285]

---

283. 115 N.Y. 506 (1889).
284. CARDOZO, THE NATURE OF THE JUDICIAL PROCESS, *supra* note 1, at 40–41.
285. 347 U.S. 483 (1954).

for example, did not expressly overrule the holding of *Plessy v. Ferguson*[286] which had authorized the enforced segregation of railroad cars. Instead, the original decision in *Brown* had a more limited scope: "We conclude that in the field of public education the doctrine of 'separate but equal' has no place."[287] Nevertheless, in subsequent *per curiam* decisions the Supreme Court struck down state-sponsored segregation of public beaches, golf courses, buses, etc., citing *Brown v. Board of Education*.[288]

Furthermore, although a lower court has no power to overrule the decision of a higher court, it may be unclear to the lower court whether or not the higher court still recognizes the original decision as authoritative. In 1996, in *Hopwood v. Texas*,[289] the Fifth Circuit Court of Appeals held that the Supreme Court had silently but effectively overruled *Regents of the University of California v. Bakke*[290] by subsequent decisions of the Supreme Court striking down affirmative action programs outside the educational setting.[291] The Fifth Circuit guessed wrong. In 2003 the Supreme Court reaffirmed its holding in *Bakke* in the case of *Grutter v. Bollinger*.[292]

18. The Case Should Be Overruled

As discussed in Chapter 5, the principle of *stare decisis* militates against reversing precedent. As noted in that chapter, the leading authority defining the scope of *stare decisis* in constitutional cases

---

286. 163 U.S. 537 (1896).

287. 347 U.S. 483, 495.

288. The per curiam decisions are listed in RONALD D. ROTUNDA & JOHN E. NOWAK, 3 TREATISE ON CONSTITUTIONAL LAW, SUBSTANCE AND PROCEDURE 379 (3rd ed. 1999).

289. 78 F.3d. 932, *cert. den.* 518 U.S. 1033 (1996). This case is also discussed in the text starting at note 253.

290. 438 U.S. 265, 320 (1978). The policy arguments in Justice Powell's opinion in the Bakke case are described in Chapter 15.

291. 78 F.3d at 944.

292. 539 U.S. 306 (2003).

is the plurality opinion of Justices Kennedy, O'Conner, and Souter from *Planned Parenthood of Southeastern Pennsylvania v. Casey.*[293] The four factors considered by the plurality in deciding whether to overrule *Roe v. Wade* were the workability of the existing rule, society's reliance on the existing rule, whether the rule had been undermined by subsequent decisions, and whether the premises of fact underlying the decision had changed.[294] The three justices found that the rule from *Roe* allowing women to choose to abort a fetus before viability was clear and easily applied, that society had changed in reliance on the ruling in *Roe*, that the original holding had not been undermined by later decisions, and that no facts or understandings of fact relevant to the original decision had been proven to be incorrect. Accordingly, they voted to reaffirm *Roe.*

In *Rutan v. Republican Party,*[295] Justice Scalia proffered a somewhat different list of factors to be taken into account in deciding whether to overrule precedent: "[O]ne is reluctant to depart from precedent. But when that precedent is not only wrong, not only recent, not only contradicted by a long prior tradition, but also has proved unworkable in practice, then all reluctance ought to disappear."[296]

The strength of precedent varies from field to field. For example, courts are less likely to overrule decisions interpreting statutes than they are cases interpreting the constitution. The stated reason is that if the legislature disagrees with a judicial interpretation of a statute, it may amend the statute; accordingly, if the legislature has declined to amend the law, then the original decision probably is consistent with the intent of the legislature.[297]

---

293. 505 U.S. 833 (1992).
294. *Id.* at 854–855.
295. 497 U.S. 62 (1990).
296. *Id.* at 110–111 (Scalia, J., dissenting).
297. This concept, the doctrine of "statutory stare decisis," is discussed in more detail in Chapter 22, "Text versus Precedent."

In summary, arguments based on precedent may be attacked on the ground that the cited case is not authoritative, that it is distinguishable on the facts or on the basis of policy, or that it ought to be overruled.

CHAPTER 14

Intra-Type Attacks on Tradition Arguments

Intra-type attacks on tradition arguments may assert that there is insufficient evidence that the tradition exists, may invoke a competing tradition, or may contend that a new tradition is emerging.

19. No Such Tradition Exists

The issue in *Moore v. City of East Cleveland*[298] concerned the constitutionality of a local "single family residential" zoning ordinance that defined the "family" in such a way as to prohibit two cousins from living in the same house with their grandmother. The Supreme Court, in an opinion written by Justice Lewis Powell, struck down the ordinance on the ground that it interfered with the "deeply rooted" tradition of persons living with extended family.[299] In dissent, Justice Byron White objected to this reasoning: "What the deeply rooted traditions of the country are is arguable; which of them deserve the protection of the Due Process Clause is even more debatable."[300]

As the following section illustrates, in most cases the difficulty is not proving that a tradition exists. Instead, the problem is that there also exists a competing tradition.

---

298. 431 U.S. 494 (1977).
299. *Id.* at 503.
300. *Id.* at 549.

20. There Have Been Competing Traditions

In a famous passage from an opinion dissenting from the Supreme Court's denial of certiorari (the court's decision not to accept the case for review) in the contraception case *Poe v. Ullman*,[301] Justice Harlan recognized the possibility of conflicting traditions. He indicated that due process represents "the balance struck by this country, having regard to what history teaches are the traditions from which it developed as well as the traditions from which it broke. That tradition is a living thing."[302]

Competing traditions were also at work in *Michael H. v. Gerald D.*[303] The issue in that case was the constitutionality of a state law that conclusively presumed that the husband of a woman was the father of a child born during the marriage. The biological father (the wife's lover) challenged the presumption, and sought a ruling recognizing him as the father of his child. Justice Scalia, writing for the majority, and Justice Brennan, writing for the dissent, each invoked "tradition." Justice Brennan cited the rights of "parenthood," which are generally accorded to biological fathers.[304] Justice Scalia, on the other hand, relied upon "the historic respect—indeed, sanctity would not be too strong a term—traditionally accorded to the relationships that develop within the unitary family."[305] Justice Scalia proposed a test for choosing between competing traditions. He urged that the controlling tradition should always be "the most specific level at which a relevant tradition ... can be identified."[306]

---

301. 367 U.S. 497 (1961).
302. *Id.* at 542 (Harlan, J., dissenting).
303. 491 U.S. 110 (1989).
304. *Id.* at 141.
305. *Id.* at 123.
306. *Id.* at 127. Richard Fallon correctly identifies this as a conflict between "general" and "specific" traditions. Richard H. Fallon, Jr., *A Constructivist Coherence Theory of Constitutional Interpretation*, 100 HARV. L. REV. 1189, 1198–1199 (1987) (hereinafter *Constructivist Coherence*).

21. A New Tradition Is Emerging

The most significant judicial attack upon "tradition" in recent years is contained in the 2003 decision of the Supreme Court in *Lawrence v. Texas*,[307] which accorded constitutional protection to people who engage in gay sex. In an extensive discussion in that case the Supreme Court employed a number of arguments rebutting the "tradition" that had been at the core of the Court's decision in *Bowers v. Hardwick*. In addition to arguing that sodomy statutes had not been consistently or rigorously enforced in America, Justice Kennedy also observed that over the last half century most states had repealed laws punishing gay sex, that the medical and legal professions had recently advocated more tolerant views of homosexuality, and that in America as well as in foreign nations there was an "emerging awareness" of tolerance for gay and lesbian citizens.[308]

Accordingly, tradition arguments can be attacked by challenging the evidence supporting the existence of the tradition, by invoking a competing tradition, or by claiming that a new tradition is emerging.

---

307. 539 U.S. 558 (2003)
308. *Id.* at 568–573 (Kennedy, J.).

CHAPTER 15

Intra-Type Attacks on Policy Arguments

As noted in Chapter 7, consequentialist arguments have a more complex structure than the other forms of legal argument. To challenge a policy argument in a systematic fashion, one must separate the argument into its constituent elements: the predictive statement and the evaluative judgment. One must ask, "What is the factual prediction of the argument?" and "What is the underlying value that the argument asserts is served by the law?"

In attacking policy arguments, as with other kinds of arguments, there is a progression. The following questions suggest a pattern for challenging policy arguments.

1. Is the factual prediction accurate?
2. Is the asserted policy one of the purposes of the law?
3. Is the asserted policy sufficiently strong?
4. How likely is it that the decision in this case will serve this policy?
5. Are there other, competing policies that are also at stake?

These questions correspond to the five intra-type attacks on policy arguments that are presented below.

22. The Factual Prediction Is Not Accurate

When we speak of consequences flowing from a judicial decision, few cases can compete with *Clinton v. Jones*,[309] in which the

---

309. 520 U.S. 681 (1997).

Supreme Court refused to postpone Paula Jones' sexual harassment suit against President Bill Clinton until the completion of his term of office. The President's primary argument for delaying the suit was that to permit civil suits against sitting presidents would materially interfere with the discharge of their official duties. The Court responded to this argument by attacking the factual premise of the President's argument:

> As a factual matter, petitioner [President Clinton] contends that this particular case—as well as the potential additional litigation that an affirmance of the Court of Appeals judgment might spawn—may impose an unacceptable burden on the President's time and energy, and thereby impair the effective performance of his office. Petitioner's predictive judgment finds little support in either history or the relatively narrow compass of the issues raised in this particular case. In the more than 200-year history of the Republic, only three sitting Presidents have been subjected to suits for their private actions. If the past is any indicator, it seems unlikely that a deluge of such litigation will ever engulf the Presidency. As for the case at hand, if properly managed by the district Court, it appears to us highly unlikely to occupy any substantial amount of petitioner's time."[310]

It was the president's untruthful responses to Ms. Jones' lawsuit, of course, that led eventually to his impeachment by the House of Representatives. In hindsight, it seems apparent that the Supreme Court underestimated the potential effects of permitting civil suits against sitting presidents.

---

310. *Id.* at 701–702.

23. The Policy Is Not One of the Purposes of the Law

Of the five ways to attack policy arguments, this is the most difficult one to master. When your opponent makes a policy argument, you may challenge it by asking a simple question: "Is this policy one of the purposes of the law?" This seemingly straightforward question masks the complex relationship between rules and policies, a relationship illustrated by the following metaphor.

Rules of law are like marker buoys that guide our course. Most people think that this is what the law is: determinate rules of conduct. But just as buoys are secured by unseen anchors, rules of law are justified by the policies they serve. Every rule serves a purpose,[311] and whenever you attempt to interpret a rule of law it is necessary to identify the purpose of the rule.[312]

---

311. "[I]t is true that a body of law is more rational and more civilized when every rule it contains is referred articulately and definitely to an end which it subserves, and when the grounds for desiring that end are stated or are ready to be stated in words." Holmes, *Path, supra* note 19, at 1000–1001.

312. The notion that the key to interpreting the law lies in identifying the purpose of the law was articulated by Sir Edward Coke over four hundred years ago. In *Heydon's Case*, 76 Eng. Rep. 637 (1584), Coke proposed that in interpreting statutes judges should take into account the following factors:

1st. What was the common law before the making of the act.
2nd. What was the mischief and defect for which the common law did not provide.
3d. What remedy the Parliament hath resolved and appointed to cure the disease of the commonwealth.
And, 4th. The true reason of the remedy; and then the office of all the Judges is always to make such construction as shall suppress the mischief, and advance the remedy, and to suppress subtle inventions and evasions for continuance of the mischief, and pro privato commodo, and to add force and life to the cure and remedy, according to the true intent of the makers of the Act, pro bono publico.

Id. at 638.

In asserting a policy argument, an attorney is not free to simply assert *any* policy that may serve his or her purposes.[313] Nor are policy arguments an invitation to courts to interpret the law in accordance with their own personal preferences. When a policy argument is presented as a *legal* argument, it is necessary to prove that the underlying policy is one that the *law* is supposed to serve. Specifically, the "evaluative" portion of a policy argument must reflect a policy choice that is fairly attributable to the law in question. For example, in *People v. Gibbons*, the case that is presented in Chapter 8, the court attributed the policy choice in favor of protecting privacy to the framers of the statute, citing evidence of this policy both in the text of the law and its legislative history. Similarly, when Justice Robert Jackson stated that an implicit purpose of the Commerce Clause was that "every farmer and every craftsman shall be encouraged to produce by the certainty that he will have free access to every market in the nation,"[314] he attributed the choice to the framers of the Constitution: "Such was the vision of the Founders...."[315]

A policy choice may be derived from more than one original source of law. For example, the doctrine of checks and balances has been inferred from the text and structure of the constitution,[316]

---

313. "Bobbitt's notion of the modalities as practice must be built upon an assumption that not every type of policy assertion is legal argument." Gene R. Nichol, *Constitutional Judgement*, 91 MICH. L. REV. 1107, 1114 (1993).

314. H.P. Hood & Sons v. Du Mond, 336 U.S. 525, 539 (1949).

315. *Id.*

316. The system of checks and balances is textually manifest in the President's power to veto Congressional enactments, Art. I, sec. 7, cl. 2; the Senate's power to reject the President's nominees to federal court or as principal officers, Art. II, sec. 2, cl. 2; the Senate's power to refuse to ratify treaties negotiated by the President, *id.*; and the power of the House of Representatives to impeach and the Senate to remove the President, Vice-President, other civil officers, and federal judges for the commission of high crimes and misdemeanors. Art. 1, sec. 5, cl. 6, and Art. II, sec. 4.

from contemporaneous evidence of the framers' intent,[317] from explicit holdings of the Supreme Court,[318] and from the way our nation's government has been conducted for two hundred years.[319] The evaluative portion of a policy argument is always derived from one of the other four types of legal argument. The policy that the law serves must arise from text, intent, precedent, or tradition. The persuasiveness of a policy argument thus depends in part upon the kind and extent of the evidence offered to prove that the policy is fairly derived from one of these sources.

Policy arguments may serve abstract values such as liberty and equality, instrumental concerns such as economic efficiency or criminal deterrence, or targeted societal goals such as improving the nutritional value of food or streamlining traffic flow. A quarter of a century ago Professor Ronald Dworkin distinguished between "principles" and "policies."[320] According to Dworkin, principles protect rights while policies foster goals. Principles are derived from reason while policies are achieved by societal force. Principles legitimately form the basis for judicial decisionmaking, while policies are the prerogative of the legislature to enact.[321] The difference between principles and policies, for Dworkin, is the difference between individual rights and collective goals: "Arguments of princi-

---

317. As James Madison observed in The Federalist Number 51, "Ambition must be made to counteract ambition." THE FEDERALIST PAPERS, *supra* note 65, at 262.

318. "Although the resolution of specific cases has proved difficult, we have derived from the Constitution workable standards to assist in preserving separation of powers and checks and balances. These standards are by now well accepted." United States v. Lopez, 514 U.S. 549, 575 (1995) (Rehnquist, J.) (citations omitted).

319. *See* Justice Frankfurter's reasoning in Youngstown Sheet & Tube v. Sawyer, quoted *supra* in the text accompanying note 116, stating that "deeply embedded ways of conducting government" act as a gloss upon the Constitution.

320. Ronald Dworkin, *Hard Cases*, 88 HARV. L. REV. 1057 (1975).

321. *Id.* at 1067–1073.

ple are arguments intended to establish an individual right; arguments of policy are arguments intended to establish a collective goal."[322]

In contrast to Dworkin, I propose that courts may legitimately construct policy arguments from either individualistic or collective values so long as the value is one that is drawn from the text of the law, the intent of its drafters, judicial precedent, or tradition. Policies that cannot be traced to one of these sources are not a policy of the law, and cannot form the basis of the evaluative portion of a policy argument.

An example of an opinion rejecting the evaluative portion of a policy argument is Justice Scalia's separate concurring opinion in the "nude dancing" case *Barnes v. Glen Theatre*.[323] In finding that there was no First Amendment right to perform or view nude dancing, Scalia wrote, "There is no basis for thinking that our society has ever shared the Thoreauvian 'you-may-do-what-you-like-so-long-as-it-does-not-injure-someone-else' beau ideal—much less for thinking that it was written into the Constitution."[324]

A closely related method of attacking a policy argument in constitutional cases is to suggest that the *asserted* purpose of the law was not the *actual* purpose, and that the actual purpose was an invalid purpose such as animus towards an unpopular group. This method of attacking the underlying policy of a law appears in a number of cases decided under the Equal Protection Clause. Justice Stevens ruled that a city's asserted purpose in refusing to grant a variance for a group home was not what it purported to be: "The record convinces me that this permit was required because of the irrational fears of neighboring property owners rather than for the protection of the mentally retarded persons who would reside in

322. *Id.* at 1067.
323. 501 U.S. 560 (1991).
324. *Id.* at 574–575. One could respond that the founders of our nation considered "liberty" and "the pursuit of happiness" to be inalienable rights.

[the] home."[325] On similar grounds, Justice Brennan invalidated an amendment to the food stamp program that denied eligibility to unrelated persons who reside together: "[T]he legislative history ... indicates that the amendment was intended to prevent so-called 'hippies' and 'hippie communes' from participating in the food stamp program."[326] Justice Kennedy came to a similar conclusion about an amendment to the Colorado Constitution that prohibited municipalities from enacting gay rights legislation: "We must conclude that Amendment 2 classifies homosexuals not to further a proper legislative end but to make them unequal to everyone else."[327]

Identifying the policy behind a law is a crucial step in the analysis. Only when the purpose of the law has been identified is it possible to proceed to the subsequent steps in attacking a policy argument: evaluating the strength of the policy, determining whether the policy will be served, and comparing the policy to competing policies.

24. The Policy Is Not Sufficiently Strong

In constitutional cases, the Supreme Court has developed a spectrum of ends-means tests for evaluating the constitutionality of governmental acts: strict scrutiny, intermediate scrutiny, and the rational basis test. These represent different standards for measuring the sufficiency of the policy analysis supporting the law. The governmental policy must be "compelling" to pass strict scrutiny, "substantial" to pass intermediate scrutiny, and merely "legitimate" to pass the rational basis test. To apply these standards one must first identify all of the governmental interests, and then determine whether any of those interests justify the law under the relevant standard.

---

325. Cleburne v. Cleburne Living Centers, Inc., 473 U.S. 432, 455 (1985).
326. U.S. Department of Agriculture v. Moreno, 413 U.S. 528, 534 (1973).
327. Romer v. Evans, 517 U.S. 620, 635 (1996).

In *Regents of the University of California v. Bakke*,[328] Justice Powell determined that a race-based affirmative action college admissions program had to meet the requirements of strict scrutiny. He observed that there were four policies offered in support of the admissions program: remedying historical discrimination generally, remedying specific, identified acts of discrimination, improving the delivery of health care services to underserved communities, and promoting educational diversity within the university. He then stated, "It is necessary to decide which, if any, of these purposes is substantial enough to support the use of a suspect classification."[329] He concluded that the goal of remedying historical, societal discrimination was not "compelling" enough to justify an affirmative action program.

25. The Policy Is Not Served in This Case

This is essentially a *causation* argument. It assumes that the asserted policy is legitimate, but it disputes that there is any causal nexus between the law and the policy goal. Justice Powell also employed this argument in *Bakke*: "Petitioner identifies, as another purpose of its program, improving the delivery of health-care services to communities currently underserved.... But there is virtually no evidence in the record indicating that petitioner's special admissions program is either needed or geared to promote that goal."[330]

In *Craig v. Boren*,[331] the Supreme Court determined the constitutionality of an Oklahoma law that prohibited the sale of beer to males (but not females) between the ages of 18 and 21. The state's policy was to discourage drunk driving, a problem that it noted was far more serious in young men than in young women. However, Justice Brennan found that the law did not closely serve the

---

328. 438 U.S. 265 (1978).
329. 438 U.S. 265, 306 (Powell, J.).
330. *Id.* at 310.
331. 429 U.S. 190 (1976).

stated purpose: "[T]he relationship between gender and traffic safety becomes far too tenuous to satisfy *Reed's* requirement that the gender-based difference be substantially related to achievement of the statutory objective."[332]

26. The Policy Is Outweighed by a Competing Policy

This is the most intricate type of intra-type attack on policy arguments. When there are competing policies at stake, the comparison between them will turn upon a complex balancing of the *weight* of the competing values and the *likelihood* that these values will be served.[333]

To return to the metaphor used earlier in this chapter, just as a buoy may be secured by more than one anchor, laws may serve more than one policy; in fact, that is usually the case. The law of tort, for example, seeks to compensate victims, deter misconduct, and promote economic efficiency, and the specific rules of the law of tort depend upon the relative weight accorded to these disparate goals. Similarly, the law of Separation of Powers is torn between

---

332. *Id.* at 204 (Brennan, J.).

333. One scholar describes the process of evaluating weight and likelihood as follows:

> Each case decided in favor of a plaintiff or a defendant resolves a conflict of interest by hierarchically ordering the goals pitted against each other in the dispute.... An examination of the law will show that the decisions of the courts and the effects of legislation result in a fairly consistent ordering of our values. The prevention of physical harm, for example, is ranked higher and more important than the prevention of economic loss.... In particular, an examination of the goal matrix of the law will show that whenever one ordering of a pair of conflicting goals will maximize only the first goal at the extreme expense of the second, while the converse ordering will maximize the second goal and produce only a minimal interference with the first, the law will generally prefer the second ordering.

J.C. Smith, *Machine Intelligence, supra* note 277, at 326, 327 (1998).

the goal of allowing each branch of government the leeway to perform its assigned function, and the goal of curbing each branch's power through an effective system of checks and balances. Another example of this tension between competing policies is present in every case where a law is challenged for being in violation of the Constitution. In every constitutional case, two fundamental principles are at war with each other: the principle that our government is subject to constitutional limitations, and the principle of majority rule.[334]

Justice Steven Breyer is perhaps the foremost judicial advocate of balancing on the current Supreme Court. In the case of *Denver Area Educational Telecommunications Corp. v. F.C.C.*,[335] which is discussed at length in Chapter 20, Justice Breyer employed a balancing approach to resolving the First Amendment issues that were presented. Justice Breyer stated: "The First Amendment interests involved are therefore complex, and require a balance between those interests served by the access requirements themselves ... and the disadvantage to the First Amendment interests of cable operators and other programmers...."[336] In contrast, Justice Kennedy has "expressed misgivings about judicial balancing under the First Amendment."[337]

The balancing of policies is also a key element in the development of the common law. In Chapter 7, there is an example of judicial

---

334. Alexander Bickel called this particular clash of principles "the countermajoritarian difficulty," and described it as follows: "[W]hen the Supreme Court declares unconstitutional a legislative act or the action of an elected executive, it thwarts the will of representatives of the actual people of the here and now; it exercises control, not in behalf of the prevailing majority, but against it." ALEXANDER M. BICKEL, THE LEAST DANGEROUS BRANCH 16–17 (1962).

This "difficulty" arises because in our nation the Constitution is law that is binding on government. Marbury v. Madison, 5 U.S. 137 (1803).

335. 518 U.S. 727 (1996).

336. *Id.* at 743 (1996) (Breyer, J.).

337. *Id.* at 784 (Kennedy, J., concurring in part and dissenting in part).

balancing from the law of Contracts,[338] and in Chapter 13 there is an example from the law of Wills.[339]

On the surface, law seems to be a set of determinate rules, but under the surface, the law is derived from and justified by myriad values and interests. These values and interests are often conflicting; the law represents a compromise among the pull of their competing aims.[340] Comparing the relative strength of these values and interests is a principal means of evaluating policy arguments.

In summary, there are five ways to attack a policy argument. One can challenge the accuracy of the factual prediction; one can challenge the legitimacy, strength, or likelihood of achieving the policy goal; or one can assert a competing policy.

---

338. *See* the excerpt from Unico v. Owen in the text accompanying notes 185–186 *supra.*

339. *See* Justice Cardozo's description of the underlying policy analysis in Riggs v. Palmer in the text accompanying notes 283–284 *supra.*

340. James Gordley notes: "The attempt to derive rules from … supposedly neutral principles has a notorious habit of leading nowhere. For if no human purposes were deemed more valuable than others, there would be no way to decide what sorts of liberty or equality to protect. Legal rules typically settle conflicts between one citizen's pursuit of his purposes and another's pursuit of his own." James Gordley, *Legal Reasoning: An Introduction*, 72 Calif. L. Rev. 138, 143 (1984).

CHAPTER 16

Cross-Type Arguments

In the Socratic dialogues written or recorded by Plato, Socrates debated the nature of abstract principles such as "courage" (*Laches*), "friendship" (*Lysis*), "virtue" (*Meno*), or "knowledge" (*Theaetetus*). Socrates' method in each dialogue was to question his opponent about the definition and source of each principle. In each case, the dialogue revealed that the opponent possessed a number of different understandings of each concept, and that these different understandings were often contradictory. Socrates' invariable conclusion was that his conversant therefore did not understand the concept.[341] In what may be an appropriate reminder to law teachers, the scholar I. F. Stone reminds us that the Socratic deconstructive teaching technique could be simply destructive: "Socrates was the master of a negative dialectic that could destroy any and every definition or proposition put to him. But he rarely offered a definite proposition of his own."[342]

Legal argument is similar to Socratic dialog in that we are attempting to define abstract concepts—the rules of law. And like courage, friendship, virtue, and knowledge, the law does not spring

---

341. "For Socrates, if you couldn't define something with unvarying comprehensiveness, then you really didn't know what it is." I.F. STONE, THE TRIAL OF SOCRATES 68 (1989). Stone accuses Socrates and Plato of "gross oversimplification and the search for absolute abstractions where there are only complex realities." Id. at 49. Thus Socrates and Plato, in their search for pure and absolute definitions, are similar to those who adhere to "foundational" legal analysis, and who reject a pluralistic understanding of law. Foundational analysis is discussed in Chapter 17.

342. *Id.* at 56.

from a single source. Law is a stew that is "brewed daily in the cauldron of the courts," and the staple fare of legal education—the
grist for the mill of the Socratic method—is the cross-type argument. "Cross-type arguments" arise when one type of legal argument is set against an argument of a different type. Cross-type
arguments present classic examples of hard cases. These are cases
where informed people of good will legitimately differ as to what
the law is, because different legal arguments yield legitimate and
different answers to questions of law.

   Cross-type arguments take two forms. First, one may assert that
one type of argument is legitimate and that the competing type of
argument is illegitimate. Second, one may assert that one type of
argument categorically or contextually outweighs an argument of
a different type. The first strategy, that of denying the legitimacy of
one or more types of arguments, is called a "foundational argument," while we may refer to the second type of cross-type attack
as a "relational argument." Each kind of cross-type argument is
considered in the following chapters.

CHAPTER 17

Foundational Cross-Type Arguments

Foundational or "privileged factor" theories assert that only certain kinds of arguments are valid; as a result, they deny the legitimacy of other kinds of argument.[343]

Foundational theories attempt to define or justify the law in terms of a single modality or interpretive device. Adherents of foundational theories contend that the law is legitimately based upon one method of interpretation. Such theories have the advantage of increased predictability and determinism, but the disadvantage of such theories is that they accept only one conception of justice as valid. Pluralistic theories like the one presented in this book, on the other hand, recognize that there are different, and often contradictory, conceptions of justice, and that these different conceptions are reflected in the different types of arguments. As Justice Felix Frankfurter observed, "[T]here is hardly a question of any real difficulty before the Court that does not entail more than one so-called principle."[344] For pluralists the law is inherently indeter-

---

343. Philip Bobbitt has observed that foundational arguments are attacks on the legitimacy of a legal argument: "An attack on these modalities is an attack on the legitimacy of the decisions they support." BOBBITT, CONSTITUTIONAL INTERPRETATION, *supra* note 2 at 108. The legal scholar Richard Fallon calls this type of argument a "privileged factor" theory: "Privileged factor theories give determinative significance to arguments within one or two of the categories and virtually ignore the other kinds of arguments." Fallon, *Constructivist Coherence*, *supra* note 306, at 1209.

344. FELIX FRANKFURTER, OF LAW AND MEN 43 (1956). H.L.A. Hart agrees:

minate because valid but contradictory legal arguments potentially exist regarding the interpretation of the law.

A famous example of a foundational argument—an argument whose premise is that the opposing argument is not simply unpersuasive, but is illegitimate—is at the core of the debate between Justice Black and Justice Frankfurter in *Adamson v. California*.[345] The constitutional question presented in *Adamson* was whether it was a violation of the Due Process Clause of the Fourteenth Amendment for a prosecutor in a criminal case to comment on the fact that the defendant had not testified in his own behalf and for the jury to take the silence of the defendant into account in determining guilt. In the opinion of Justice Frankfurter, the Due Process Clause requires the court to determine the overall "fairness" of the trial. He stated that the Due Process Clause "imposes upon this Court an exercise of judgment upon the whole course of the proceedings in order to ascertain whether they offend those canons of decency and fairness which express the notions of justice of English-speaking peoples...."[346] He concluded in his concurring opinion that it did not violate "those canons of decency and fairness" for the prosecutor to comment on the silence of the accused or for the jury to infer guilt from it.

In dissent, Justice Hugo Black argued that the framers intended to incorporate the Fifth Amendment's "right to silence" into the Due Process Clause of the Fourteenth Amendment, and that the defendant's conviction would therefore have to be reversed. But

---

It is of crucial importance that cases for decision do not arise in a vacuum but in the course of the operation of a working body of rules, an operation in which a multiplicity of diverse considerations are continuously recognized as good reasons for a decision.... Frequently these considerations conflict, and courts are forced to balance or weigh them and to determine priorities among them.

H.L.A. Hart, *Problems of Philosophy of Law*, 6 ENCYCLOPEDIA OF PHILOSOPHY 271 (Paul Edwards, ed. 1967).

345. 332 U.S. 46 (1947).

346. *Id.* at 67 (Frankfurter, J., concurring).

Justice Black did not simply say that his textual and original intent arguments were more persuasive than Justice Frankfurter's balancing approach. Instead, he contended that Frankfurter's legal argument was illegitimate:

> This decision reasserts a constitutional theory spelled out in *Twining v. New Jersey*, that this Court is endowed by the Constitution with boundless power under "natural law" periodically to expand and contract constitutional standards to conform to the Court's conception of what at a particular time constitutes "civilized decency" and "fundamental liberty and justice." I would not reaffirm the *Twining* decision. I think that decision and the "natural law" theory of the Constitution upon which it relies degrade the constitutional safeguards of the Bill of Rights and simultaneously appropriate for this Court a broad power which we are not authorized by the Constitution to exercise.... [347]

Like Justice Black, Justice Scalia is a textualist who has mounted foundational arguments. In *Michael H. v. Gerald D.*,[348] he asserted that "a rule of law that binds neither by text nor by any particular, identifiable tradition, is no rule of law at all."[349] Consistent with his devotion to text and tradition to the exclusion of other methods of analysis, Justice Scalia has ridiculed the concept of legislative intent: "[t]o tell the truth, the quest for the 'genuine' legislative intent is probably a wild-goose chase anyway."[350] Justice Scalia rejects the

---

347. 332 U.S. 46, 69.

348. 491 U.S. 110 (1989).

349. *Id.* at 127 (footnote 6) (1989). Justice Brennan responded, "In a community such as ours, 'liberty' must include freedom not to conform. The plurality today squashes this freedom by requiring specific approval from history before protecting anything in the name of liberty." *Id.* at 141.

350. Scalia, *Judicial Deference, supra* note 36, at 517. *See also* ANTONIN SCALIA, A MATTER OF INTERPRETATION: FEDERAL COURTS AND THE LAW 29 (1997) (hereinafter A MATTER OF INTERPRETATION).

use of legislative history in the interpretation of statutes, contending that legislative history "is much more likely to produce a false or contrived legislative intent than a real one,"[351] and that the intent of Congress "is best sought by examining the language that Congress used."[352] Justice Scalia has evidently had an impact on the reasoning of the Supreme Court. Over the past two decades, the Court's reliance on legislative history has steadily declined.[353] Another example of foundational analysis is the "originalism" of Robert Bork. Bork rejected policy analysis in the interpretation of the Constitution as illegitimate because it is not a "neutral principle,"[354] and he would rely almost exclusively on the theory of "original intent." Bork takes this position because he believes that popular sovereignty—the will of the people—is the single overriding value that the law should serve. He considers other types of legal arguments to be inconsistent with the principle of democracy.

Foundationalism is not limited to conservative jurists. Justice Black usually rejected policy arguments in favor of textual arguments in order to *expand* individual rights, as he did in *Adamson*.

---

351. SCALIA, A MATTER OF INTERPRETATION, *supra* note 350, at 32. Professor Adrian Vermeule agrees with Scalia that to maximize certainty and predictability the courts should not consider legislative history in determining the meaning of statutes, and also suggests that the courts should pick and stay with one canon of construction rather than using competing canons, and should observe a strict rule of statutory stare decisis. Adrian Vermeule, *Interpretative Choice*, 75 N.Y.U. L. Rev. 74, 128–148 (2000).
352. Moskal v. United States, 498 U.S. 103, 130 (Scalia, J. dissenting).
353. *See* Michael H. Koby, *The Supreme Court's Declining Reliance on Legislative History: The Impact of Justice Scalia's Critique*, 36 HARV. J. ON LEGIS. 369 (1999) (graphing a dramatic reduction in the number and proportion of citations to legislative history between 1980 and 1998). Justice Breyer, in contrast to Justice Scalia, is an "avid supporter" of the use of legislative history. *Id.* at 374.
354. *See* Bork, *Neutral Principles*, *supra* note 64, at 8, 17 (1971); *see also* RAOUL BERGER, GOVERNMENT BY JUDICIARY: THE TRANSFORMATION OF THE FOURTEENTH AMENDMENT 364 (1977).

Similarly, in *Roth v. United States*[355] Justice Black concurred in Justice Douglas' dissenting opinion, in which they took a literal, textual approach to obscenity cases. Justice Douglas stated: "The First Amendment, its prohibition in terms absolute, was designed to preclude courts as well as legislatures from weighing the values of speech against silence."[356] In addition, a critic of Justice Scalia contends that the courts should reject arguments based on tradition because tradition "favors majoritarianism over individual rights, encourages social conformity, fuses social biases and prejudices into the Constitution, and fails to constrain judicial discretion.... [I]t is clear that ... these interpretive techniques merely mask substantive political values that the Justice holds."[357] A more measured response to a foundational argument based upon "tradition" is not to reject tradition altogether, but to observe that it is not the *only* valid type of legal argument. As Justice Kennedy has stated, "history and tradition are the starting point but not in all cases the ending point" of constitutional analysis."[358]

There are many legal scholars who agree with Philip Bobbitt that foundational arguments are "fundamentally flawed."[359] As Professor Akhil Amar says, "No tool of interpretation is a magic bullet,"[360]

---

355. 354 U.S. 476 (1957).

356. *Id.* at 514.

357. David Schultz, *Scalia on Democratic Decision Making and Long Standing Traditions: How Rights Always Lose*, 31 SUFFOLK U. L. REV. 319, 348 (1997).

358. County of Sacramento v. Lewis, 523 U.S. 833, 857 (1998), *quoted in* Lawrence v. Texas, 539 U.S., at 572.

359. *See* Bobbitt, *Reflections*, *supra* note 22, at 1872. Paul McGreal agrees: "[C]onstitutional scholars from such varied positions as Laurence Tribe and Robert Bork have, at one time or another, joined the hunt for a grand theory of constitutional law.... This article takes a contrary view: The Constitution does not require or prefer any particular theory of constitutional interpretation." Paul E. McGreal, *Ambition's Playground*, 68 FORDHAM L. REV. 1108 (2000). The pluralistic model of law is also consistent with Paul Wangerin's emphasis on "multiplicity" in legal education. See Wangerin, *supra* note 4.

360. Amar, *Intratextualism*, *supra* note 3, at 801.

and as Professors Eskridge and Frickey say, "Each criterion is relevant, yet none necessarily trumps the others."[361] This country rejected foundational analysis when the Senate voted not to confirm Robert Bork.[362] Foundational analysis is unsatisfactory because each type of argument serves an important value that the law is bound to take into account. Cross-type arguments that take these values into account, and that compare the strength of one type of argument against the strength of another type of argument, are called relational arguments. While foundational arguments attack the legitimacy of legal arguments, relational arguments attack their weight. Relational arguments are described generally in the next chapter, and are discussed in detail in the chapters that follow it.

---

361. Eskridge and Frickey, *Practical Reasoning, supra* note 2, at 352.

362. Bobbitt observed that: "For fifteen years Robert Bork had been attacking the legitimacy of the means of judicial reasoning that undergirded the Warren Court decisions. To this campaign, in part, he owed his public reputation, his nomination, and ultimately his defeat." BOBBITT, CONSTITUTIONAL INTERPRETATION, *supra* note 2, at 102.

CHAPTER 18

Relational Cross-Type Arguments

Some legal scholars have said that cross-type conflicts cannot be resolved in an honest and rational way because the different types of legal arguments are "incommensurable,"[363] like apples and or-

---

363. Phillip Bobbitt, the legal scholar who first identified the modalities of constitutional interpretation, contended that the different types of legal arguments are "incommensurable." BOBBITT, CONSTITUTIONAL INTERPRETATION, *supra* note 2, at 116, 155–162. Bobbitt proposed that we treat conflicts between the different modalities as if they were moral problems. "In the very incommensurabilities of the forms of argument lies the possibility of moral choice." *Id.* at 161. He proposed that conflicts between the incommensurable modalities can be resolved only by recourse to "conscience:" "The United States Constitution formalizes a role for the conscience of the individual sensibility by requiring decisions that rely on the individual moral sensibility when the modalities of argument clash." *Id.* at 168.

The obvious problem with Bobbitt's solution to the commensurability problem is that it is not a *legal* solution but a *moral* one. A number of scholars have criticized Bobbitt's proposal. "It is far from self evident that the exercise of conscience is consistent with — or guarantees — justice." Dennis Patterson, *Truth in Law: A Modal Account*, LAW AND TRUTH 128, 149 (Dennis Patterson, ed. 1996) (hereinafter *Truth in Law*). "Bobbitt thinks that judges should decide these cases in the way that their personal ultimate values imply is most desirable." Richard S. Markovits, *Legitimate Legal Argument and Internally-Right Answers to Legal-Rights Questions*, 74 CHI.-KENT L. REV. 415, 445 (1999). Bobbitt's solution was characterized as a "conversation stopper." Nichol, *Constitutional Judgement*, *supra* note 309, at 1115. Other scholars have referred to Bobbitt's conception of conscience as "a black box:" "Conscience for Bobbitt seems to be largely a black box; the heart may have its reasons, but they are not otherwise sub-

anges. My response to this argument is, "Would you rather eat an apple or an orange?"

Legal arguments *can* be compared to each other. There is a measuring rod for determining the relative persuasiveness of different legal arguments. The standard of persuasiveness is found in the values that underlie each of the different types of legal argument. Courts implicitly or explicitly weigh these values whenever they compare one type of argument against another.

In Chapter 2, when the different types of legal argument were introduced, I suggested that each type of argument serves a different fundamental value of our system of laws. Textual analysis makes the law objective. Reference to the intent of the drafters of the law shows respect for the principle of popular sovereignty. Following precedent ensures stability in the law. Adhering to tradition promotes social cohesion. And policy arguments allow the law to adjust to new situations and ensure that the consequences of the legal determination will be consistent with the underlying purposes of the law.

In the passage quoted in the introduction of this book and repeated below, Benjamin Cardozo eloquently posed the question of how to balance these values:

> What is it that I do when I decide a case? To what sources of information do I appeal for guidance? In what proportions do I permit them to contribute to the result? In what proportions ought they to contribute? If a precedent is applicable, when do I refuse to follow it? If no precedent is applicable, how do I reach the rule that will make a precedent for the future? If I am seeking logical consistency, the symmetry of the legal structure, how far shall I seek it? At what point shall the quest be halted by some discrepant custom, by some consideration of

---

ject to rational examination...." Balkin & Levinson, *Constitutional Grammar, supra* note 209, at 1796.

the social welfare, by my own or the common standards of justice and morals? Into that strange compound which is brewed daily in the cauldron of the courts, all these ingredients enter in varying proportions.[364]

The resolution of cross-type conflict—and the solution to the commensurability problem—lies in balancing the values that each of the different types of argument serve.[365] It is not possible to create a rigid hierarchy of types of arguments.[366] There is a rough sense

---

364. CARDOZO, THE NATURE OF THE JUDICIAL PROCESS, *supra* note 1, at 10.

365. This is consistent with the suggestion of William Eskridge and Phillip Frickey that the resolution of hard cases depends upon the exercise of "practical reason." Eskridge and Frickey, *Practical Reasoning*, *supra* note 2, at 351–352. In response, Larry Alexander has stated, "I think the claims on behalf of such practical reason are hogwash." Alexander, *The Banality of Legal Reasoning*, *supra* note 100, at 521. Kent Greeenawalt discusses this strategy of balancing the value of different interpretive techniques of statutory interpretation in GREENAWALT, 20 QUESTIONS, *supra* note 31, at 59–76. The balancing of these underlying values may also be consistent with the suggestion of Edward Adams and Daniel Farber that the courts use "fuzzy logic" to resolve difficult questions of interpretation. Edward S. Adams & Daniel A. Farber, *Beyond the Formalism Debate: Expert Reasoning, Fuzzy Logic, and Complex Statutes*, 52 VAND. L. REV. 1243 (1999).

366. Richard Fallon was one of the first legal scholars to identify the "commensurability problem:" "Constitutional law has a commensurability problem. The problem arises from the variety of kinds of argument that now are almost universally accepted as legitimate in constitutional debate and interpretation." Fallon, *Constructivist Coherence*, *supra* note 304, at 1189.

Fallon also proposed a solution to the problem. He suggested that the incommensurability problem may be resolved by resort to a hierarchy among constitutional modalities: "Sometimes...the strongest arguments within the different categories will point irreversibly to different conclusions. In such cases,...[t]he implicit norms of our constitutional practice...require that the claims of the different kinds of arguments be ranked hierarchically." *Id.* at 1286. Fallon ranks constitutional arguments in the following order: text, intent, structural argument, precedent, and value arguments. *Id.* at 1193–1194. For example, in the case of a conflict between text and intent, he concludes: "When arguments from text and from the

that the arguments should be ranked in the order they are listed: text, intent, precedent, tradition, and policy.[367] Certainly many judicial opinions proceed in that order.[368] However, the existence of a rigid hierarchy could not explain why, for example, when text conflicts with intent, the text controls in some cases, and the intent of the drafters controls in other cases.[369] Each conflict must be evaluated in the context of the particular case.

The resolution of cross-type conflicts is more nuanced and complex than can be explained by either a foundational or hierarchical approach. Cross-type conflicts are resolved by balancing the policies that are served by the different kinds of legal arguments.[370] For ex-

---

framers' intent prove resistant to accommodation, their hierarchical authority demands recognition. And while the range of permissible accommodations is broad, the hierarchical ordering of categories of argument presumes that there are limits." *Id.* at 1282.

Fallon's hierarchy has been criticized for being "admittedly intuitive and somewhat hesitant." Stephen M. Griffin, *Pluralism in Constitutional Interpretation*, 72 TEX. L. REV. 1753, 1764 (1994). Phillip Bobbitt observes that Fallon's hierarchy creates a regression problem: "If there is a hierarchy of modes, which mode supports this hierarchy?" BOBBITT, CONSTITUTIONAL INTERPRETATION, *supra* note 2, at 156.

367. Virtually all legal scholars who have proposed pluralistic models of legal reasoning list the types of argument in roughly the same order. It is also similar to the order that Paul Wangerin suggests for the organization of a brief in note 206 *supra*.

368. For example, the dissenting opinion in People v. Gibbons, reprinted in Chapter 8, expressly cites text, intent, and precedent, in that order.

369. In the next chapter, "Text versus Intent," it becomes apparent that in some cases text controls intent, while in others intent takes precedence over the text of the law.

370. Professor Fallon acknowledged that "by accommodating the claims to interpretive authority of five factors," a pluralistic model of law "respects the values underlying all of them." Fallon, *Constructivist Coherence*, *supra* note 304, at 1250. Similarly, Fallon characterizes balancing theories as having "intuitive plausibility," (*id.* at 1227–1228), but ultimately concludes that such theories suffer from the defects that courts do not expressly balance one form of legal argument against another, and that the interdependence of legal arguments militates against balancing. *Id.* at

ample, in cases where the court finds that the need for objectivity and clarity outweighs the need to conform to societal expectations, then text will prevail over tradition. In a case that pitted precedent against policy, Cardozo balanced "consistency and certainty" against "equity and fairness," and found that the latter prevailed.[371] This is typical of the balancing process that is inherent to resolving cross-type conflicts. As H.L.A. Hart said:

> No doubt because a plurality of such principles is always possible it cannot be demonstrated that a decision is uniquely correct: but it may be made acceptable as the reasoned product of informed impartial choice. In all this we have the "weighing" and "balancing" characteristic of the effort to do justice between competing interests.[372]

Balancing these underlying values is made even more difficult by the fact that the relative strength of each type of argument varies from field to field. For example, the doctrine of *stare decisis* is generally acknowledged to be stronger when we interpret statutes than when we interpret the Constitution.[373] Similarly, the principle of

---

1229–1230. By "interdependence," Fallon is referring to the fact that the forms of argument are often mixed. *Id.* at 1238. When legal arguments are bimodal or polymodal the "commensurability problem" is of course made more complex.

371. Jacob & Youngs v. Kent, 230 N.Y. 239, 242–243, 129 N.E. 889, 890 (1921). This case is extensively discussed in Chapter 20.

372. H.L.A. Hart, *Problems of Philosophy of Law, supra* note 344, at 271.

373. The reduced role for the doctrine of stare decisis in constitutional interpretation is a phenomenon of the twentieth century, according to one scholar:

> Thus, the prevailing doctrine of stare decisis at the time of the framing and throughout the nineteenth century generally rejected the notion of a diminished standard of deference to constitutional precedent. When Justice Brandeis (dissenting in *Burnet*) sought to lay claim to a purportedly longstanding position of the Court that constitutional cases should readily be corrected where

intent is stronger in cases of statutory interpretation than it is in cases interpreting the Constitution. There are three reasons for these differences in the interpretation of statutes and the constitution. First, statutes can be easily amended. If the legislature disagrees with a court's interpretation of a statute, all it needs to do is to amend the law. It is vastly more difficult to amend the Constitution when the people disagree with a decision of the Supreme Court. Second, the intent of the framers of the Constitution is more remote, less accessible, and possibly less pertinent than the intent of the legislature that enacted a statute. The lapse of time has made it more difficult to prove the intent of the framers of Constitution, and may have made their intent less relevant. Third, the Constitution is broadly worded and is intended to endure for generations. For example, interpreting the Due Process Clause requires the courts to determine what is "fundamentally fair," and the Equal Protection Clause makes it necessary to determine whether two groups of people are "similarly situated." These determinations are sensitive to context, are susceptible to differences of opinion, and have evolved in response to changes in society. As a result, it is not surprising that both precedent and intent arguments are stronger in the interpretation of statutes than for constitutional questions.

Furthermore, the weight given to a category of argument may also depend upon the facts of the specific case. In one case, societal reliance may loom large, influencing the court to follow text, precedent, or tradition. In another case in the same field of law, the variety and unpredictability of factual circumstances may make policy arguments a more attractive means of resolving the question of law.

---

they are found inconsistent with reason, the Court's actual position on that point had been to treat constitutional precedent in the same way it treated other decisions. Despite its questionable historical pedigree, Brandeis' approach has been unquestioningly adopted by the modern Court.

Thomas R. Lee, *Stare Decisis in Historical Perspective: From the Founding Era to the Rehnquist Court*, 52 Vand. L. Rev. 647, 727 (1999).

Each type of legal argument has particular virtues and vices which vary from case to case and from field to field. The solution that I propose to the "commensurability problem" is that judges implicitly weigh not only the internal strength of an argument on its own terms, but also the external strength of the type of argument as measured by the underlying values of objectivity, popular will, consistency, societal coherence, flexibility and justice, in the context of the particular case. The persuasiveness of any legal argument is a function of both its internal (intra-type) and its external (cross-type) strength.

Cross-type conflict is the principal source of "hard cases." Hard cases are by definition cases where the law is indeterminate, where plausible arguments can be constructed for either side,[374] and where able judges may, in good faith, come to different conclusions about what the law is.[375]

---

374. Several legal scholars agree with this definition of a hard case. "In hard cases, two or more legitimate modalities will conflict." BOBBITT, CONSTITUTIONAL INTERPRETATION, *supra* note 2, at xiv. "Reasonable, respectable legal arguments often are available on both sides of such legal issues, which is just what makes them 'hard.'" David Lyons, *Justification and Judicial Responsibility*, 72 CALIF. L. REV. 178, 182 (1984). "The fact that in 'hard' cases we can construct plausible arguments in support of contradictory conclusions would seem to show that no deductively valid argument can be constructed in support of either conclusion." Brian Winters, *Logic and Legitimacy: The Uses of Constitutional Argument*, 48 CASE WESTERN L. REV. 263, 277 (1998). "In easy cases, most of the evidence points in the same direction and is thereby mutually reinforcing. In the hard cases, however, the evidence points in different directions...." Eskridge and Frickey, *Practical Reasoning*, *supra* note 2, at 322–323.

375. Robert Bork considers "indeterminacy" to be the central problem in constitutional law, and he developed his theory of originalism as a solution to that problem. "Certainly, Bork deserves high praise for his brilliant insights and for his effort to find certainty in the Constitution. But his quest for certainty continues, while others, such as Cardozo, Coke, Corbin, and Wilson have taken a more pragmatic approach and 'have become reconciled to the nature of uncertainty, because [they] have grown to see it as inevitable.'" Paul Brickner, *Robert Bork's Quest for Certainty: Attempting to Reconcile the Irreconcilable*, 17 J. CONTEMP. L. 49, 66 (1991), quoting CARDOZO, THE NATURE OF THE JUDICIAL PROCESS, *supra* note 1,

A convenient way to organize examples of cross-type disputes is by the type of conflict that is presented. In the following chapters I present commonplace examples of cross-type conflicts, including text versus intent, precedent versus policy, text versus policy, and text versus precedent.

---

at 166–167. A century ago Justice Holmes warned of the danger of believing that a system of law "can be worked out like mathematics from some general axioms of conduct.... I once heard a very eminent judge say that he never let a decision go until he was absolutely sure that it was right. So judicial dissent often is blamed, as if it meant simply that one side or the other were not doing their sums right, and if they would take more trouble, agreement inevitably would come." Holmes, *Path, supra* note 19, at 998. *See also* Kent Greenwalt, *Discretion and Judicial Decision: The Elusive Quest for the Fetters that Bind Judges*, 75 COLUM. L. REV. 359 (1975); and Eskridge and Frickey, *Practical Reasoning, supra* note 2, at 380.

CHAPTER 19

Text versus Intent

This chapter presents examples of conflicts between the text of the law and what the drafters intended. This is a common pattern of cross-type conflict, and it is not a new one. A century ago, Oliver Wendell Holmes and the noted legal scholar John Wigmore debated the relative merits of text and intent. Holmes thought that we ought to interpret the law according to the plain meaning of the legal text rather than according to the intent of someone who drafted the text: "[W]e ask, not what this man meant, but what those words would mean in the mouth of a normal speaker of English...."[376] In contrast, John Wigmore considered the intent of the drafters to be more relevant than the "plain meaning" of the text: "[T]he 'plain meaning' is simply the meaning of the people who did *not* write the document."[377]

The conflict between text and intent is receiving increased attention from legal scholars,[378] and there is still substantial dis-

---

376. Oliver Wendell Holmes, *The Theory of Legal Interpretation*, 12 HARV. L. REV. 417, 417–418 (1899).

377. JOHN H. WIGMORE, 9 EVIDENCE 198 (James H. Chadbourn rev. 1981).

378. A seminal article on this conflict is Eskridge's *The New Textualism*, *supra* note 35. See also Jonathan R. Siegel, *Textualism and Contextualism in Administrative Law*, 78 B.U. L. REV. 1023, 1025–1032, (1998) (hereinafter *Textualism and Contextualism*) (contrasting textualism and intentionalism); Antonin Scalia, *The Rule of Law as a Law of Rules*, 56 U. CHI. L. REV. 1175 (1989); and Martin H. Redish and Theodore T. Chung, *Democratic Theory and the Legislative Process; Mourning the Death of Originalism in Statutory Interpretation*, 68 TUL. L. REV. 803, 817–831 (1994). Redish and Chung propose a compromise between the two positions which they call "textualist originalism." *Id.* at 859.

agreement about their relative priority. Professor Kent Greenawalt suggests that in extreme cases intent may control plain legal text: "Somewhat more controversially, judges may also be justified in rejecting a straightforward reading of the text if it is clearly at odds with the underlying statutory purpose, is manifestly absurd, or is undoubtedly unjust."[379] Professor Larry Alexander, in contrast, contends that unambiguous text takes precedence over intent: "[O]ne can make authorial intentions the touchstone of authoritative meanings so long as those meanings are not inconsistent with conventional understandings of the words."[380]

The conflict between text and intent arises from a fundamental disagreement over what the law is. Professor Alexander poses the question cogently: "What is a statute? Knowing what a statute is—whether, for example, a statute is what the lawmakers intended to accomplish by their words (what they meant by them), or alternatively is what those marks signify conventionally as words in a particular language—precedes knowing what the statute means."[381]

---

379. GREENAWALT, 20 QUESTIONS, *supra* note 31, at 57 (1999). See Sinclair, *Statutory Reasoning, supra* note 191, at 345–346, for an example of a case where "[c]lear and demonstrable legislative intent trumped clear and undisputed statutory language." Robert Keeton also discusses cases where the Supreme Court discerned statutory purposes which were not apparent from the text of the law. Robert Keeton, *Statutory Analogy, Purpose, and Policy in Legal Reasoning: Live Lobsters and a Tiger Cub in the Park*, 52 MD. L. REV. 1192, 1201–1203 (1993).

380. Larry Alexander, *The Banality of Legal Reasoning, supra* note 100, at 520–521 (1998). However, Alexander and Sherwin recently suggested that intent takes priority over text, stating: "In our view, however, the objective of authoritative settlement dictates that the only meaning that should count as the meaning of [the lawgiver's] rules is the meaning [the lawgiver] intended the rules to have." LARRY ALEXANDER AND EMILY SHERWIN, THE RULE OF RULES: MORALITY, RULES, AND THE DILEMMAS OF LAW 98 (2001).

381. Larry Alexander, *Incomplete Theorizing: A Review Essay of Cass R. Sunstein's Legal Reasoning and Political Conflict*, 72 NOTRE DAME L. REV. 531, 544 (1997).

A classic case of conflict between text and intent arose in the case of *Green v. Bock Laundry Machine Co.*,[382] which was briefly described in Chapter 3. In that case the United States Supreme Court was faced with a difficult question concerning the meaning of Evidence Rule 609(a)(1), which provided in part that, "for the purpose of attacking the credibility of a witness, evidence that the witness has been convicted of a crime shall be admitted...only if...the court determines that the probative value of admitting this evidence outweighs its prejudicial effect to the defendant...." The reason for the rule is that, in a criminal case, if the jury learns that the defendant has previously been convicted of a serious crime, it may be tempted to find the defendant guilty not because the evidence proves his guilt, but because of his criminal record. The question in *Green* was whether this rule applied in *civil* cases as well as *criminal* cases. The Court rejected a "plain meaning" approach to interpreting the rule: "The Rule's plain language commands weighing of prejudice to a defendant in a civil trial as well as in a criminal trial. But that literal reading would compel an odd result in a case like this."[383] Instead, the Court based its interpretation of Evidence Rule 609 upon an exhaustive examination of its legislative history.[384] The court concluded: "Had the conferees desired to protect other parties or witnesses, they could have done so easily....They did not for the simple reason that they intended that only the accused in a criminal case should be protected from unfair prejudice by the balance set out in Rule 609(a)(1)."[385]

Thus, in *Green* the Court gave primacy to the intent of the law over its text. In another sharp conflict between text and intent, however, a California court construed the evidence of intent narrowly in order to give effect to the text of the law. In *Story Road Flea Market, Inc. v. Wells Fargo Bank*,[386] the issue concerned the liability of Wells Fargo Bank to its customer, which was a flea mar-

---

382. 490 U.S. 504 (1989).
383. *Id.* at 509.
384. *See id.* at 515–524.
385. *Id.* at 523–524.
386. 42 Cal.App.4th 1733 (1996).

ket that had a checking account at the bank. A thief forged the drawer's signature to several of the flea market's checks, and cashed the checks at the bank. A key issue in the case was how to measure the bank's responsibility to check for forged signatures. Is the bank held to a "professional standard" (the customary procedures followed by other banks) or is it subject to a "reasonableness standard" (the procedures that a jury finds is reasonable under the circumstances)?

The relevant statute, Section 3-103(a)(7) of the Uniform Commercial Code, sets up a professional standard. It provides that banks that process checks have not breached their duty of "ordinary care" if "the bank's prescribed procedures do not vary unreasonably from general banking usage." The Official Comment to this section, however, establishes a reasonableness standard with regard to the handling of checks. The comment says: "Nothing in Section 3-103(a)(7) is intended to prevent a customer from proving that the procedures followed by a bank are unreasonable, arbitrary, or unfair." Under the "reasonableness" test the bank might be liable to its customer for paying the forged checks even if the bank's procedures complied with general banking usage, if the jury found that these procedures were unreasonable.

The court addressed this conflict by stating that the wording of the comment applies only to "an action where the fairness of bank procedures is relevant,"[387] and it found that fairness was not relevant in actions based on forged signatures.[388] The reasoning of the court has been criticized on the ground that the language of the comment obviously *does* apply to actions based on forged signatures.[389] The court in *Story Road* failed to confront the blatant in-

---

387. *Id.* at 1745.
388. *Id.*
389. This aspect of the decision in *Story Road* is sharply criticized in Rochelle L. Wilcox, *Ordinary Care Under the Code: A Look at the Evolving Standard of Bank Liability Under U.C.C. 4-406*, 1997 UTAH L. REV. 933 (1997). Wilcox concludes:
    Had it been the drafters' intention to establish that compliance

consistency between the language of the statute and the language of the official comment.

In choosing between the text of the law and the intent of its framers, a court is essentially choosing between the need for objectivity and clarity in determining what the law is, and the desire to give effect to the will of the people who enacted the law. In *Story Road*, the court found that the text of the Commercial Code was determinative, perhaps in order to promote predictability in the field of commercial relations. In *Green*, the court apparently believed that it was more important to conduct trials in the way that the drafters of the Rules of Evidence intended, rather than to blindly apply the plain meaning of the law.

The same conflict between text and intent also arises in the context of the interpretation of contracts as well: "One goal of contract law is to enforce contracts as written so as not to 'jeopardize the certainty of contractual duties which parties have a right to rely on.'... But contract law has other, competing goals as well. One such goal is to interpret and enforce contracts in light of the reasonable expectations the parties had at the time the contract was made."[390]

In the following chapter, which is mainly devoted to cases exhibiting the conflict between precedent and policy, there is also an example of the conflict between text and intent in the interpretation of a contract.

---

with general banking practice relative to signature verification processes was the exercise of ordinary care as a matter of law, the drafters could easily have limited the unambiguous language of the last sentence. Their failure to do so, when it was clearly an issue of which they were aware, leads to the conclusion that they did not intend to do so.

Id. at 951.

390. *Warner, supra* note 278, at 1540, quoting Southern Concrete Services, Inc., v. Mableton Contractors, 407 F. Supp. 581, 584 (N.D. Ga. 1975). See also Nicholas M. Insua, *Dogma, Paradigm, and the Uniform Commercial Code: Sons of Thunder v. Borden Considered*, 31 RUTGERS L. J. 249 (1999) (arguing against a "plain meaning" approach to the interpretation of contracts).

CHAPTER 20

Precedent versus Policy

In cases where legal text is absent or where its meaning is unclear both on its face and in the record of its adoption, two other modes of analysis often assume prominence: case law and policy analysis. In these situations, hard cases frequently arise because of a conflict between precedent and policy. In this chapter I discuss two striking examples of this kind of cross-type conflict: the contracts case *Jacob & Youngs v. Kent*,[391] and the First Amendment case *Denver Area Educational Telecommunications Corp. v. F.C.C.*[392]

1. Jacob & Youngs v. Kent

Jacob & Youngs, Inc. v. Kent is an old chestnut of the law of contracts.[393] The majority opinion was written by Justice Benjamin Cardozo when he served on the New York State Court of Appeals.

Jacob & Youngs was a building contractor who built a house for Kent, the owner. When the house was finished the owner refused to pay the remaining amount that was owed on the contract. The owner claimed that he did not owe the contractor the full purchase price because the contract had called for the installation of one type of pipe (Reading pipe), and the contractor had substituted another

391. 230 N.Y. 239, 129 N.E. 889 (1921).
392. 518 U.S. 727 (1996).
393. *Jacob & Youngs* is a standard tool of legal pedagogy. It is reprinted in 11 out of 13 leading contracts casebooks. Cunningham, *Cardozo and Posner: A Study in Contracts, supra* note 1, at 1459.

type of pipe without the owner's permission. The contractor claimed that the substitution was accidental, and that the pipe that was used was just as good as Reading pipe.

The contractor sued for the unpaid portion of the purchase price, but it faced two hurdles. First, the contractor had to convince the court that it had "substantially performed" the contract. Second, it had to convince the court that it should recover the full purchase price. The New York Court of Appeals agreed with the contractor on both counts.

In deciding the first issue, Justice Cardozo created a "multi-factor test" for determining whether a contractor has "substantially performed" a contract. The four factors identified by Justice Cardozo were "the purpose to be served, the desire to be gratified, the excuse for deviation from the letter, [and] the cruelty of enforced adherence."[394] In balancing these considerations, Justice Cardozo found that the contractor had substantially performed the contract. Cardozo acknowledged that this multi-factor standard was relatively indeterminate as compared to a rule requiring "exact performance" of a contract, but he vigorously argued that the standard was justified because considerations of "equity and fairness" outweighed "consistency and certainty."

> Those who think more of symmetry and logic in the development of legal rules than of practical adaptation to the attainment of a just result will be troubled by a classification where the lines of division are so waver-

---

394. *Id.* The Restatement, Second, of Contracts quickly adopted Cardozo's factors for determining whether or not the contractor had substantially performed the contract. "This doctrine of substantial performance is one of Cardozo's most important contributions to the law of contracts, having been showcased in a Restatement section soon after it was handed down and having been widely adopted ever since." Cunningham, *supra* note 1, at 1442. See also Amy B. Cohen, *Reviving Jacob & Youngs, Inc. v. Kent: Material Breach Doctrine Reconsidered*, 42 VILL. L. REV. 65, 78–79 (1997).

ing and blurred. Something, doubtless, may be said on the score of consistency and certainty in favor of a stricter standard. The courts have balanced such considerations against those of equity and fairness, and found the latter to be the weightier.[395]

The second issue in *Jacob & Youngs* was, "How much of an allowance or deduction from the contract price was the owner entitled to on account of the contractor's failure to install the correct brand of pipe?" Since most of the pipe had already been encased in the walls, it would have been prohibitively expensive to replace it with Reading pipe.[396] If the owner's allowance were the cost of replacing the non-conforming pipe, the contractor would have no recovery. On the other hand, if the owner's allowance were the difference between the value of the house with the pipe that was used and the value that the house would have had if Reading pipe had been installed—an amount that the court stated was "either nominal or nothing"[397]—then the contractor would be entitled to all or virtually all of the remainder of the unpaid contract price.

Here, Cardozo was apparently constrained by precedent. In a previous case, *Spence v. Ham*,[398] the New York Court of Appeals had specified the measure of damages, holding that in cases of sub-

395. 230 N.Y. 239, 242–243, 129 N.E. 889, 891. One scholar cites this as "an example of the on-going dialectic, in general contract law, between the use of the 'rule of law' to advance the norms of certainty and predictability and the 'ex contractu' norms of fairness and justice that favor ad hoc exceptions or the use of standards in place of rules." Larry A. Di-Matteo, *The Norms of Contract: The Fairness Inquiry and the "Law of Satisfaction"—A Nonunified Theory*, 24 HOFSTRA L. REV. 349 (1995).

396. "The plumbing was then encased within the walls except in a few places where it had to be exposed. Obedience to the order meant more than the substitution of other pipe. It meant the demolition at great expense of substantial parts of the completed structure." 230 N.Y. 239, 240–241, 129 N.E. 889, 890.

397. *Id.* at 244, 129 N.E. 889, 891.

398. 163 N.Y. 220, 57 N.E. 412 (1900).

stantial performance the contractor was entitled to recover the contract price less the cost of completing the contract according to its terms.[399] However, Cardozo chose not to follow precedent. Instead he created an exception to *Spence*, and held that where a contract has been substantially performed, and the cost of completing the contract strictly according to its terms is substantially disproportionate to "the good to be attained,"[400] the owner's allowance is to be measured by the difference in value between the promised performance and the actual performance, rather than by the cost of completing the contract strictly according to its terms. Cardozo stated: "It is true that in most cases the cost of replacement is the measure. Spence v. Ham, supra. The owner is entitled to the money which will permit him to complete, unless the cost of completion is grossly and unfairly out of proportion to the good to be attained. When that is true, the measure is the difference in value."[401]

In support of this ruling Cardozo explained that the same policy considerations supporting the substantial performance doctrine also supported this liberal measure of recovery for the contractor: "The rule that gives a remedy in cases of substantial performance with compensation for defects of trivial or inappreciable importance has been developed by the courts as an instrument of justice. The measure of the allowance must be shaped to the same end."[402]

Accordingly, Cardozo resolved the conflict between precedent and policy by weighing the necessity for predictability against considerations of justice. In this case, he determined that principles of equity and fairness outweighed considerations of consistency and certainty.

For similar reasons Cardozo chose to emphasize "the intent of

---

399. The court stated in Spence: "Unsubstantial defects may be cured, but at the expense of the contractor, not of the owner." *Id.* at 226, 57 N.E. 410, 413.

400. 230 N.Y. 239, 244, 129 N.E. 889, 891.

401. *Id.*

402. *Id.* at 245, 129 N.E. 889, 892.

the parties" over the "plain meaning" of the contract. Although the contract explicitly stated that in cases of less than full performance the owner was entitled to deduct the cost of completion from the contract price,[403] Justice Cardozo ruled that the law would be "slow to impute the purpose" of imposing a forfeiture on the contractor, "where the significance of the default is grievously out of proportion to the oppression of the forfeiture."[404]

In the next case, just as in *Jacob & Youngs*, the court was called upon to weigh considerations of consistency and certainty against principles of equity and fairness.

2. Denver Area Educational Telecommunications Consortium v. F.C.C.

Another case that illustrates the conflict between precedent and policy is the decision of the Supreme Court in *Denver Area Educational Telecommunications Consortium, Inc. v. F.C.C.*,[405] a First Amendment case. The conflict in this case between precedent and policy arose because changes in telecommunications technology made it necessary to reexamine how the principles of freedom of speech apply to the medium of cable television.

In 1992 Congress enacted the Cable Television Consumer Pro-

---

403. RICHARD DANZIG, THE CAPABILITY PROBLEM IN CONTRACT LAW: FURTHER READINGS ON WELL-KNOWN CASES 109–110 (1978).

404. 230 N.Y., at 243–244, 129 N.E., at 891.

405. 518 U.S. 727 (1996). For additional discussion of the background and reasoning of the Denver Area case, *see The Supreme Court 1995 Term: Restrictions on Indecent Cable Programming*, 110 HARV. L. REV. 246 (1996); Diana Israelashvili, *A Fear of Commitment: The Supreme Court's Refusal to Pronounce a First Amendment Standard for Cable Television in Denver Area Educational Telecommunications Consortium, Inc. v. FCC*, 71 ST. JOHN's L. REV. 173 (1997); and Charles Nesson & David Marglin, *The Day the Internet Met the First Amendment: Time and the Communications Decency Act*, 1996 HARVARD JOURNAL OF LAW & TECH. 113, 118–119 (1996).

tection and Competition Act, which provided in part that cable television operators could prevent "indecent" programs from being shown on the "leased access" channels of their cable systems.[406] The Supreme Court held that this portion of the law was constitutional, but there was no majority opinion, only a collection of plurality, concurring, and dissenting opinions. Not only did the justices of the Supreme Court disagree about the result; the justices also disagreed about whether to use precedent or policy arguments to interpret the First Amendment.

Justice Thomas (who concurred in upholding the law) and Justice Kennedy (who dissented) both favored using precedent to resolve this case, but they disagreed about which precedent to follow. Justice Kennedy argued that cable television is like a "public forum" or a "common carrier." In other words, cable television is a medium that people have a right to use to express themselves.[407] In such a setting, Justice Kennedy observed, the rights of speakers and listeners predominate. According to Justice Kennedy, the people who produce television programs and the viewers who wish to see such programs have constitutional rights that must be taken into account, while the operator of the cable network performs the merely mechanical function of keeping the system running, and has no First Amendment rights that are at stake.[408] Accordingly, Justice Kennedy, relying on the precedent of the "public forum" cases, found that the Act was unconstitutional.

---

406. 518 U.S. 727, 732.

407. Justice Kennedy stated: "Laws requiring cable operators to provide leased access are the practical equivalent of making them common carriers, analogous in this respect to telephone companies: They are obliged to provide a conduit for the speech of others." *Id.* at 796.

408. Justice Kennedy said: "For purposes of these cases, we should treat the cable operator's rights in these channels as extinguished, and address the issue these petitioners present: namely, whether the Government can discriminate on the basis of content in affording protection to certain programmers. I cannot agree with Justice Thomas that the cable operator's rights inform this analysis." *Id.*

Justice Thomas thought that a different line of cases was applicable. He considered cable television to be like a newspaper, and he analogized the cable operator to the publisher of a newspaper.[409] A newspaper publisher clearly has the right to decide whether or not to publish an article submitted by an author, while the author and the reading public have no constitutional right to demand that the author's article be published. By invoking the cases that established the rights of newspaper publishers, Justice Thomas found that the rights of cable operators predominate, and that programmers and viewers have no rights that need to be taken into account.[410] As a result, Justice Thomas held that the law allowing the cable operator to exclude indecent programming was constitutional.

Justice Breyer took a different approach altogether in deciding this case. He criticized Justices Kennedy and Thomas for relying so extensively on precedent to decide this case. Instead, Justice Breyer made a policy argument to uphold the law. Justice Breyer first identified all of the values and interests that were at stake. These included the interest of the government in protecting children from programs containing depictions of sex, violence, and bad language, the right of adult viewers to have access to such programs, the right of programmers to produce such material, and the right of cable operators to control access to their cable systems. The test that Justice Breyer used was to "closely scrutiniz[e] [the law] to assure that it properly addresses an extremely important problem, without imposing, in light of the relevant interests, an unnecessarily great restriction on speech."[411] After balancing "the interests of programmers,

<hr/>

409. *Id.* at 816.
410. Justice Thomas stated: "None of the petitioners in these cases are cable operators; they are all cable viewers or access programmers or their representative organizations. It is not intuitively obvious that the First Amendment protects the interests petitioners assert, and neither petitioners nor the plurality have adequately explained the source or justification of those asserted rights." *Id.* at 817 (citations to the record omitted).
411. *Id.* at 743.

viewers, cable operators, and children,"[412] Justice Breyer held that the law was constitutional.

Perhaps the most compelling portions of the justices' opinions are where they attempt to justify the approach they each took to deciding the case. For example, Justice Kennedy criticized Justice Breyer's policy approach for its lack of predictability. Kennedy stated that "[t]he plurality opinion...is adrift,"[413] and that the test used by Justice Breyer would "sow confusion in the courts."[414] Justice Breyer countered this criticism by explaining why it was inappropriate for Justice Kennedy and Justice Thomas to rely on precedent:

> Both categorical approaches suffer from the same flaws: they import law developed in very different contexts into a new and changing environment, and they lack the flexibility necessary to allow government to respond to very serious political problems without sacrificing the free exchange of ideas the First Amendment is designed to protect.[415]

Furthermore, Justice Breyer faulted the reasoning of Justices Kennedy and Thomas because their analysis was limited. Each of the other justices took into account only *some* of the rights and interests that were at stake. Justice Kennedy considered only the rights of programmers and viewers, while Justice Thomas considered only the rights of cable operators. In contrast, Justice Breyer's free-

---

412. *Id.* at 750.
413. *Id.* at 780.
414. *Id.* at 786. Justice Thomas, who concurred in the judgment with Justice Breyer, nevertheless joined Justice Kennedy's criticism of Breyer's analysis: "It is true that the standard I endorse lacks the 'flexibility' inherent in the plurality's balancing approach, but that relative rigidity is required by our precedents and is not of my own making." *Id.* at 818.
415. *Id.* at 740.

wheeling balancing approach allowed him to consider the rights and interests of *all* of the parties.[416]

In summary, in cases where legal text is not controlling, a common kind of cross-type conflict pits precedent versus policy. *Jacob & Youngs v. Kent* and *Denver Area* are instructive because each case contains an explicit discussion of the relative merits of each type of argument. In those cases Justice Cardozo and Justice Breyer elevated policy over precedent. Both found fault with existing rules that failed to adequately balance the interests and values that were at stake. Both gave reasons for their interpretive choice,[417] and both were criticized by dissenting justices who would have given priority to precedent.

---

416. Justice Breyer wrote: "While we cannot agree with Justice Thomas that everything turns on the rights of the cable owner, we also cannot agree with Justice Kennedy that we must ignore the expressive interests of cable operators altogether." *Id.* at 747.

417. Professor Adrian Vermeule coined the term "interpretive choice" to describe this problem: "[T]he problem is one of 'interpretive choice' — the selection of one interpretive doctrine, from a group of candidate doctrines, in the service of a goal specified by a higher-level theory of interpretation." Vermeule, *supra* note 351, at 76.

CHAPTER 21

Text versus Policy

Cross-type conflicts between text and policy arise in diverse fields of law. In some cases the courts give effect to the language of the constitution or statute in spite of compelling policy arguments, while in other cases the policy considerations trump textual interpretations. This chapter features cases from both Commercial Law and Constitutional Law.

1. Text versus Policy in the Law of Negotiable Instruments

When a check is stolen and the thief forges the indorsement of the true owner (the payee), the owner of the check may sue to recover the amount of the check. But who is liable to the owner? In *Denn v. First State Bank*,[418] the Minnesota Supreme Court was called upon to determine whether the owner of the check could sue the depositary bank (the bank that allowed the thief to deposit the stolen check into the thief's checking account). At the time of the decision, a provision of the Uniform Commercial Code stated that a depositary bank that acted "in good faith and in accordance with reasonable commercial standards" was not liable in conversion to the true owner of the check.[419]

---

418. 316 N.W.2d 532 (Minn. 1982).

419. "[A] representative, including a depositary or collecting bank, who has in good faith and in accordance with the reasonable commercial standards applicable to the business of such representative dealt with an

But there was a compelling policy argument in favor of imposing liability on the depositary bank. The Code allowed the owner
of the check to sue the payor bank (the bank on whom the check
was written) for conversion, and the payor bank could then sue the
depositary bank for breach of warranty. Accordingly, it would be
far more efficient—it would avoid circuity of action—to allow the
owner of the check to recover directly from the depositary bank.
The Minnesota Supreme Court cited a decision by the California
Supreme Court (*Cooper v. Union Bank*[420]) and a decision by a Pennsylvania trial court (*Ervin v. Dauphin Trust Co.*[421]) that held that
this policy of efficiency was powerful enough that the law ought to
be interpreted to permit the owner of the check to sue the depositary bank. Despite the force of this reasoning, the Minnesota
Supreme Court felt constrained by the text of the U.C.C. to dismiss the case against the depositary bank. The Minnesota Supreme
Court said:

> The arguments of the *Ervin* and *Cooper* courts are per-
> suasive, but we are compelled to reach an opposite con-
> clusion. We can ignore neither the plain language of the
> statute which expressly includes depositary and col-
> lecting banks in its description of representatives nor
> the comments which appear to exclude such banks from
> liability.[422]

The *Denn* case may be contrasted to the decision of the federal
district court in *United States Fidelity & Guaranty Co. v. Federal Reserve Bank of New York*.[423] In that case a thief had deposited a phony

---

instrument or its proceeds on behalf of one who was not the true owner
is not liable in conversion or otherwise to the true owner beyond the
amount of any proceeds remaining in his hands." Former U.C.C. 3-419.
   420. 9 Cal. 3d 371, 107 Cal. Rptr. 1 (1973).
   421. 84 Dauph. 280, 38 Pa. D.&C.2d 437 (1965).
   422. 316 N.W.2d 532, 536.
   423. 620 F.Supp. 361 (S.D. N.Y. 1985), *aff'd per curiam* 786 F.2d 77
(2d Cir. 1986).

check into his account at Fidelity. The check was fraudulently en-
coded so that it would be misrouted in the check collection process.
Fidelity sent the check through the collection process, but because
of the misencoding the check was diverted and delayed among the
collecting banks. Meanwhile, Fidelity allowed the thief to withdraw
the funds from its checking account, leaving Fidelity with the loss
when the check was finally returned unpaid with the explanation
that the check was not drawn on a real account. Some of the banks
in the collection process may have been negligent in handling the
check, but Fidelity was grossly negligent by allowing the thief to
withdraw the funds. Accordingly, the defendant banks claimed that
Fidelity should not be allowed to recover from them, because of
Fidelity's own negligence. The problem with this defense was that
although the U.C.C. expressly recognized the defense of contributory or comparative negligence in a number of other situations
arising under Article 3 of the U.C.C., the Code did not make negligence a defense in the type of lawsuit brought by Fidelity under
Article 4. The federal court stated:

> The primary difficulty with defendant's theory is that
> it is not expressly sanctioned by the U.C.C.... There is
> no express requirement that the plaintiff demonstrate
> its own due care as a prerequisite to recovery, nor is
> there any mention of comparative negligence. There is
> simply no mention of the effect, if any, of a plaintiff's
> negligence on its recovery.[424]

Nevertheless, the federal court expressly chose to elevate policy
over text:

> [T]o adhere blindly to the limitations imposed by those
> rules, if to do so would violate the policies which the

424. *Id.* at 369.

U.C.C. otherwise seeks to promote, would be unwise and unjust. Nor does the Code demand such adherence. As Judge Knapp noted in his seminal *Northpark* decision, "the history of the U.C.C. makes it abundantly clear that, especially in the context of those provisions which impose a duty of care, the Code's watchword is 'flexibility.'" I do not, therefore, find the lack of a rule of contributory or comparative negligence in Article 4 to be an insuperable barrier to defendants' claim that such a rule should be imposed.[425]

Why did the federal court choose to follow policy rather than text in the *Fidelity* case, while the Minnesota Supreme Court in *Denn* chose text over policy? The answer lies in the relative strength of the textual and policy arguments, and the comparative importance of objectivity versus flexibility in the context of each case. The text was clearer in *Denn* than in *Fidelity*, while the policy in *Fidelity* (denying recovery to someone who contributed to the loss) was stronger than the policy in *Denn* (judicial economy). In *Denn* the need for objectivity outweighed the competing policy consideration, while in *Fidelity* the reverse was true.

2. Text versus Policy in Separation of Powers Cases

In Separation of Powers cases the classic division on the Supreme Court has been between those justices who reason from text and those who rely upon policy analysis. Constitutional scholars refer to this as the conflict between "formalism" and "functionalism."[426] This pattern

---

425. *Id.* at 369, quoting Northpark National Bank v. Bankers Trust Co., 572 F. Supp. 524, 533 (S.D.N.Y. 1983).

426. This term was coined by Professor Peter L. Strauss in *Formal and Functional Approaches to Separation-of-Powers Questions — A Foolish Inconsistency?*, 72 CORNELL L. REV. 488 (1987). More recent commentary on this topic may be found in William N. Eskridge, Jr., *Relationships Between*

first emerged in *Youngstown Sheet & Tube v. Sawyer*[427] (the "Steel Seizure Case"), which arose when Harry Truman ordered his Secretary of Commerce to assume control of the nation's steel mills to avoid a labor strike during the Korean War.

Justice Hugo Black utilized a textual approach to evaluate the legality of the President's action under the Constitution. Justice Black stated that the Constitution prevented President Truman from seizing the steel mills because this would constitute the presidential exercise of legislative power in violation of Art. I, sec. 1, which vests "all legislative powers" in the Congress. Black stated: "[T]he Constitution is neither silent nor equivocal about who shall make laws which the President is to execute."[428]

Justice Robert Jackson concurred in Justice Black's opinion, but he took a radically different approach to deciding the case. First, Justice Jackson stated that the case could not be decided by defining the terms "legislative power" and "executive power." Jackson said: "The actual art of governing under our Constitution does not and cannot conform to judicial definitions of the power of any of its branches based on isolated clauses or even single Articles torn from context."[429] In rejecting Black's textual approach, Jackson was essentially arguing that the terms "legislative power" and "executive power" are not mutually exclusive — that there are no watertight compartments into which all governmental functions may be subdivided. Jackson observed: "Presidential powers are not fixed but fluctuate, depending upon their disjunction or conjunction with those of Congress."[430] Justice Jackson thus dispensed with a textual approach, because the ambiguity of the constitutional provisions precluded a definitive result. Jackson also found that neither

Formalism and Functionalism in Separation of Powers Cases, 22 Harv. J. L. & Pub. Pol'y 21 (1998).

427. 343 U.S. 579 (1952).
428. *Id.* at 587.
429. *Id.* at 635.
430. *Id.* at 635.

intent[431] nor precedent[432] provided reliable guidance to the court. He was left with policy arguments, and he constructed two arguments that have had profound influence on this area of the law. First, Jackson argued that the purpose of the doctrine of Separation of Powers is to allow the creation of "a workable government."[433] In other words, the Constitution is not simply a theoretical model of an ideal government, but is a blueprint for a government that can actually function. Second, he constructed a theory of interaction between the President and Congress under which the President's power was greatest "[w]hen the President acts pursuant to an express or implied authorization of Congress,"[434] and is at its lowest ebb "[w]hen the President takes measures incompatible with the expressed or implied will of Congress."[435] Justice Jackson ultimately concluded that President Truman was disabled from seizing the steel mills because he had acted in the face of Congressional disapproval.[436] Jackson's approach emphasized policy considerations, in contrast to Justice Black's effort to resolve the case by textually defining the relevant terms of the Constitution.

This pattern of conflict between "formalism" and "functionalism" has been repeated in subsequent separation of powers cases. In *INS v. Chadha*[437] and *Bowsher v. Synar*,[438] the United States

---

431. Justice Jackson stated: "Just what our forefathers did envision or would have envisioned had they foreseen modern conditions, must be divined from materials almost as enigmatic as the dreams Joseph was called upon to interpret for Pharaoh." *Id.* at 634.

432. Justice Jackson said: "And court decisions are indecisive because of the judicial practice of dealing with the largest questions in the most narrow way." *Id.* at 635.

433. "While the Constitution diffuses power the better to secure liberty, it also contemplates that practice will integrate the dispersed powers into a workable government." *Id.*

434. *Id.*

435. *Id.* at 637.

436. *Id.* at 640.

437. 462 U.S. 919 (1983).

438. 478 U.S. 714 (1986).

Supreme Court considered the constitutionality of political innovations that had been designed by Congress to address serious social problems. At stake in *Chadha* was the constitutionality of the
"one-house legislative veto," a mechanism that allowed either house
of Congress to reverse the decisions of administrative agencies,
while the issue in *Bowsher* concerned the constitutionality of the
Balanced Budget and Emergency Deficit Control Act of 1985, pursuant to which the Comptroller General of the United States, an
agent of Congress, was charged with the duty of balancing the federal budget. In each case the Court held that law violated the doctrine of Separation of Powers, primarily because the text of the
Constitution did not expressly permit this exercise of power by the
legislature. Chief Justice Burger's *expressio unius* argument against
the constitutionality of the one-house legislative veto is set forth
in Chapter 3. Addressing Justice White's policy argument, Justice
Burger concluded: "[The] fact that a given law or procedure is efficient, convenient, and useful in facilitating functions of the government, standing alone, will not save it if it is contrary to the
Constitution."[439]

Justice White dissented in both *Chadha* and *Bowsher* for policy
reasons. In *Bowsher*, Justice White condemned the majority's "dis-
tressingly formalistic view of separation of powers as a bar to the
attainment of governmental objectives...."[440] Justice White argued
that, in determining the constitutionality of these laws under the
Separation of Powers doctrine, the court should give priority to a
single policy consideration—preserving the system of checks and
balances. Justice White said: "[The] role of this Court should be
limited to determining whether the Act so alters the balance of authority among the branches of government as to pose a genuine
threat to the basic division between the lawmaking power and the
power to execute the law."[441]

439. 462 U.S. at 944.
440. 478 U.S. at 759.
441. *Id.* at 776.

In short, in both *Chadha* and *Bowsher* Justice Burger invoked the canon of construction *expressio unius* and found a negative implication in the Constitution against the political innovations developed by Congress. Justice White, in contrast, utilized a policy approach, and found the one-house legislative veto and the balanced budget act to be constitutional because they did not upset the balance of power between Congress and the President.

This pattern of conflict between text and intent was carried over into the case of *Morrison v. Olson*,[442] which concerned the constitutionality of the Independent Counsel Act. That law was drafted following the Watergate scandal to permit the appointment of an Independent Counsel who was not subject to Presidential control and who could investigate and prosecute crimes by leading members of the government. It was asserted that this law violated the Separation of Powers because the Independent Counsel was appointed by a special court instead of by the President and because the Congress had delegated some of the President's executive power to the Independent Counsel. Chief Justice Rehnquist, relying principally upon policy arguments, upheld the law. Using the functional approach developed by Justice White in *Chadha* and *Bowsher*, Justice Rehnquist found that the Independent Counsel Act did not "impermissibly undermine" the power of the executive branch[443] or "disrupt the proper balance between the coordinate branches."[444]

Justice Scalia dissented in part on textual grounds. Like Justice Burger, Justice Scalia drew a negative implication from the language of the Constitution, and concluded that the Independent Counsel Act invaded the "executive power" expressly vested in the President. Justice Scalia said: "Art. II, sec. 1, cl. 1 of the Constitution provides: 'The executive Power shall be vested in a President of the United States.'... [T]his does not mean *some* of the executive power, but *all* of the executive power."[445]

---

442. 487 U.S. 654 (1988).
443. *Id.* at 695.
444. *Id.*
445. *Id.* at 705.

Each of the Separation of Powers cases after *Youngstown Sheet & Tube* concerned the constitutionality of an innovative structural change in our government. The one-house legislative veto, the balanced budget act, and the independent counsel act were all new ways of conducting governmental business. The textual arguments—plain meaning and *expressio unius* arguments—were used to support the proposition that these changes in government were unconstitutional, because almost by definition a structural change in government represents something not provided for in the Constitution. In contrast, policy arguments were used to argue that the new laws were constitutional because these laws did not alter the fundamental balance of power among the branches. In general, in Separation of Powers cases the clash between textual and policy arguments mirrors the clash between those who believe that the Constitution forbids political innovation and those who believe that the Constitution permits it.

CHAPTER 22

Text versus Precedent

The Civil Procedure case of *Ankenbrandt v. Richards*[446] presents an interesting conflict between text and precedent.

The issue in *Ankenbrandt* was whether the federal courts have jurisdiction to adjudicate domestic relations cases in diversity cases.[447] The federal courts have jurisdiction in cases that involve questions of federal law (federal question cases), and in cases that are decided under state law where the plaintiff and the defendant are citizens of different states (diversity cases). The current statute governing diversity cases, which was adopted in 1948, gives the federal courts jurisdiction over "all civil actions" between citizens of different states.[448] The statute, however, was inconsistent with longstanding precedent establishing a "domestic relations exception" to diversity jurisdiction, originating with the 1858 Supreme Court decision in *Barber v. Barber*.[449] Under that case, and the cases that followed it, the federal courts had no jurisdiction to hear domestic relations cases between citizens of different states.

The majority in *Ankenbrandt* followed precedent instead of the plain language of the statute. Previous versions of the diversity-of-citizenship statute, like the current version, made no reference to a "domestic relations exception," but the federal courts had consis-

---

446. 504 U.S. 689 (1992).

447. For a discussion of this doctrine see Michael Ashley Stein, *The Domestic Relations Exception to Federal Jurisdiction: Rethinking an Unsettled Federal Courts Doctrine*, 36 B.C. L. Rev. 669 (1995).

448. 28 U.S.C. 1332.

449. 62 U.S. 582 (1858).

tently interpreted those laws as if the federal courts had no jurisdiction in domestic relations cases. The *Ankenbrandt* court thought
it particularly significant that for over a century Congress had ac-
quiesced to the courts' interpretation of a similar diversity statute
by failing to amend it:

> We thus are content to rest our conclusion that a do-
> mestic relations exception exists as a matter of statu-
> tory construction not on the accuracy of the historical
> justifications on which it was seemingly based, but rather
> on Congress' apparent acceptance of this construction
> of the diversity jurisdiction provisions in the years prior
> to 1948, when the statute limited jurisdiction to "suits
> of a civil nature at common law or in equity."[450]

The Court specifically invoked the principle of "statutory *stare
decisis*:" "Considerations of stare decisis have particular strength in
this context, where 'the legislative power is implicated, and Congress
remains free to alter what we have done.' "[451] Accordingly, the majority of the Supreme Court held that the 1948 statute, like the previous versions of the law, should be interpreted as prohibiting the
federal courts from exercising jurisdiction in domestic relations
cases.

Justice Blackmun concurred in the result, but insisted that the
majority of the court had misinterpreted the statute. He thought
that the plain meaning of the diversity-of-citizenship statute was
that the federal courts do have subject matter jurisdiction over domestic relations cases. He stated: "The diversity statute is not ambiguous at all."[452] He concluded, however, that the federal courts
were free to abstain from exercising jurisdiction in domestic relations cases.[453]

---

450. 504 U.S. 689, 700.
451. *Id.*, quoting Patterson v. McLean Credit Union, 491 U.S. 164,
172–173 (1989).
452. 504 U.S. 689, 707 (Blackmun, J., concurring).
453. *Id.* at 715.

In *Ankenbrandt*, the majority of the Supreme Court chose precedent over text, in part because they concluded that this result better reflected the likely Congressional intent. As in the cases described in the previous chapters, what made *Ankenbrandt* a hard case was the conflict among the different types of legal arguments.

CHAPTER 23

A Logical Demonstration of the Theory of the Five Types of Legal Argument

I have previously argued that pure legal reasoning cannot be expressed in logical form because so much of legal reasoning involves balancing. Policy analysis, the art of distinguishing cases, and cross-type arguments all require value judgments that cannot be performed by a system of pure logic. However, it is important to explain the role that logic *does* play in legal analysis, because when an attempt is made to reduce legal analysis to a system of logic, the five types of legal arguments are found to constitute the root premises of the analysis.

The brief of a case is, in fact, an argument of deductive logic. The four parts of a case brief – the facts, issue, statement of the law, and the holding – correlate precisely to the four elements of a logical syllogism – the minor premise, the question, the major premise, and the conclusion.[454] Here is the standard example of a syllogism of deductive logic:

QUESTION: Is Socrates mortal?

MINOR PREMISE: Socrates is a man.

---

454. *See* CESARE BECCARIA, ON CRIMES AND PUNISHMENTS 11 (David Young trans., Hackett Publ'g Co. 1986) (1764) ("In every criminal case, a judge should come to a perfect syllogism: the major premise should be the general law; the minor premise, the act which does or does not conform to the law; and the conclusion, acquittal or condemnation.").

MAJOR PREMISE: All men are mortal.

CONCLUSION: Socrates is mortal.[455]

The legal syllogism may be demonstrated with the following simple case. Where a paid hit man shoots and kills a sleeping victim, we would no doubt find the assassin guilty of murder using the following legal syllogism:

ISSUE: Is the defendant guilty of murder?

FACT: The defendant purposefully and without justification or excuse caused the death of another person.

LAW: Any person who, without justification or excuse, purposefully causes the death of another person, is guilty of murder.

HOLDING: The defendant is guilty of murder.

Legal scholars have observed, however, that the brief of a case does not consist of simply one logical syllogism, but is rather a series or chain of syllogisms.[456] The steps in the chain of legal analysis may be traced by challenging the accuracy of either the minor premise (the facts) or the major premise (the law). In the foregoing example we might challenge the major premise and ask, "Is it true that any person who purposefully and without justification or excuse causes the death of another person is guilty of murder?" This inquiry will likely lead us to a statute, and if we have accurately quoted the statute then our major premise will be upheld as a correct statement of the law. If we were to challenge the minor

---

455. Robert Schmidt has observed that this ubiquitous example of a syllogism, though commonly attributed to Aristotle, does not appear in Aristotle's writings. Robert H. Schmidt, *The Influence of the Legal Paradigm on the Development of Logic*, 40 S. Tex. L. Rev. 367, 400 fn. 32 (1999).

456. *See* Ruggiero Aldisert, Logic for Lawyers: A Guide to Clear Legal Thinking (1997); Brian Winters, *Logic and Legitimacy: The Uses of Constitutional Argument*, 48 Case Western L. Rev. 263 (1998).

premise we would ask, "Is it true that the defendant purposefully and without justification or excuse caused the death of another person?" This is quite clearly an easy question, and could be answered simply by looking to the ordinary meaning of the words of the statute and applying those meanings to the facts of the case. In short, under the "plain meaning" of the statute, we would find the defendant guilty of murder.

But we can imagine a much more difficult case. Suppose that instead of hit man the defendant is a battered spouse who has endured decades of threats and beatings, and that her abusive husband had angrily yelled that he was going to kill her and the children, just before he fell asleep on the couch, leaving his loaded gun within reach on the coffee table. Suppose she then picks up the gun and shoots and kills her sleeping husband. Now the inquiry into the minor premise becomes interesting. "Is it true that the defendant purposefully caused the death of another person?" "Is it true that the defendant acted without justification?" "Is it true that the defendant's actions are not excused?" Reasonable people might disagree upon each of these points, because legal arguments can be constructed from the text of the law, from judicial precedent, from our legal and social traditions, or from policy, that might support a finding of innocence, the existence of an affirmative defense, or a reduction of the charge to a lesser offense.[457]

The steps in the chain of logical syllogisms and the precise role of the five types of legal arguments may be further illustrated with some of the legal arguments from the case of *Marbury v. Madison*.[458] For purposes of simplification I have omitted Marshall's tradition, policy and intratextual arguments, and instead present some of his textual and intent arguments in logical form. Here are a few of the issues that were resolved by the Supreme Court in John Marshall's opinion in that case:

---

457. *See* 1 JANE CAMPBELL MORIARTY, PSYCHOLOGICAL AND SCIENTIFIC EVIDENCE IN CRIMINAL TRIALS ch. 7 (1996).
458. 5 U.S. 137 (1803).

1. Does the Supreme Court have jurisdiction over this case?
2. Does the Supreme Court have original jurisdiction to issue a writ of mandamus to the Secretary of State?
3. Is Section 13 of the Judiciary Act a valid statute?
4. Is Section 13 of the Judiciary Act in conflict with the Constitution?
5. Does Article III, Section 2, Clause 2, of the Constitution authorize Congress to grant the Supreme Court original jurisdiction to issue writs of mandamus against public officers of the United States?
6. Are statutes that are in conflict with the Constitution valid?

The reader may recognize that the foregoing issues have been arranged in rough logical order. In other words, in order to answer the first question, we must know the answer to the second question, and so on. Before we can know whether the Supreme Court has jurisdiction over this case, we must know whether there is a statute conferring such jurisdiction, and if so, we must consider whether or not this statute is valid. To determine whether the statute is valid we must find out whether this statute conflicts with the Constitution, and finally, near the beginning of the chain of syllogisms, we must determine whether or not a statute that conflicts with the Constitution is valid. I have paraphrased the syllogisms that comprise some of the reasoning that led John Marshall to the conclusion that the Supreme Court lacked jurisdiction over Marbury's plea for a writ of mandamus:

1. ISSUE: Does the Supreme Court have jurisdiction over this case?

> FACT: This is a case involving the Supreme Court's exercise of original jurisdiction to issue a writ of mandamus to the Secretary of State.

> LAW: The Supreme Court lacks original jurisdiction to issue a writ of mandamus to the Secretary of State.

> HOLDING: The Supreme Court lacks jurisdiction over this case.

2. ISSUE: Does the Supreme Court have original jurisdiction to issue a writ of mandamus to the Secretary of State?

> FACT: Section 13 of the Judiciary Act is not valid.

> LAW: The Supreme Court may exercise jurisdiction to issue a writ of mandamus to the Secretary of State only if Section 13 of the Judiciary Act is valid.

> HOLDING: The Supreme Court lacks original jurisdiction to issue a writ of mandamus to the Secretary of State.

3. ISSUE: Is Section 13 of the Judiciary Act valid?

> FACT: Section 13 of the Judiciary Act is in conflict with the Constitution.

> LAW: Statutes that are in conflict with the Constitution are not valid.

> HOLDING: Section 13 of the Judiciary Act is not valid.

4. ISSUE: Is Section 13 of the Judiciary Act in conflict with the Constitution?

> FACT: Section 13 of the Judiciary Act provides that the Supreme Court has original jurisdiction to issue writs of mandamus to officers of the United States, but the Constitution does not authorize Congress to grant the Supreme Court original jurisdiction to issue writs of mandamus to officers of the United States.

> LAW: If one law permits what another law forbids, the laws are in conflict.

> HOLDING: Section 13 of the Judiciary Act of the Constitution is in conflict with the Constitution.

5. ISSUE: Does the Constitution authorize Congress to grant the Supreme Court original jurisdiction to issue writs of mandamus to officers of the United States?

FACT: If the Constitution is interpreted as allowing Congress to grant the Supreme Court original jurisdiction to issue writs of mandamus to officers of the United States, then the second sentence of Article III, Section 2, Clause 2 would be rendered meaningless.

LAW: The Constitution may not be interpreted in such a way as to render any portion of it meaningless.

HOLDING: The Constitution does not authorize Congress to grant the Supreme Court original jurisdiction to issue writs of mandamus to officers of the United States.

6. ISSUE: Are statutes that are in conflict with the Constitution valid?

FACT: The framers intended for any statute in conflict with the constitution to be invalid.

LAW: The constitution is to be interpreted according to the intent of the framers.

HOLDING: Statutes that are in conflict with the Constitution are not valid.

Notice the links between one logical syllogism and the next. The "holding" of the Court in one step of the analysis supplies either the "fact" or the "law" in the next step of the analysis. In this case, for example, because we are tracing the reasoning of the Court back towards its root premises, the "holding" of syllogism 6 supplies the "law" of syllogism 3, and the "holding" of syllogism 5 supplies a portion of the "fact" premise of syllogism 4. The following illustration demonstrates the relation among the six syllogisms.

Syl. 5 Holding → Syl. 4 Fact
                 Syl. 4 Holding → Syl. 3 Fact
Syl. 6 Holding   →   Syl. 3 Law
                               Syl. 3 Holding → Syl. 2 Law
                                                Syl. 2 Holding → Syl. 1 Law

As we trace the reasoning of the Court back towards its original premises, we discover broader and broader principles of law that are at stake. We started by asking whether or not the Court had jurisdiction in a particular case, and we find that in order to make that determination it is necessary to determine whether or not statutes which are in violation of the Constitution are valid.

The foregoing syllogisms reveal three root premises upon which the reasoning of the Court is based. In syllogism number 4 the minor premise consists of the text of a statute and the text of the Constitution. In syllogism number 5, we find this major premise: "The Constitution may not be interpreted in such a way as to render any portion of it meaningless."[459] This is a canon of construction. And syllogism number 6 contains the major premise stating that "The Constitution is to be interpreted according to the intent of the framers," which in Marshall's words was a reflection of "the original and supreme will,"[460] that is, the will of the people.

In summary, the brief of a case represents an attempt to depict the application of law to facts in the form of an argument of deductive logic. Even though logic is inadequate to capture the essence of legal reasoning because it cannot account for balancing the value of one principle against another, we learn a valuable lesson about the law when we lay out the entire structure of a legal argument in logical form. The foregoing exercise illustrates that legal reasoning

---

459. Or, as Marshall stated, "It cannot be presumed that any clause in the constitution is intended to be without effect." 5 U.S., at 174.

460. *Id.* at 176. Marshall stated:

That the people have an original right to establish, for their future government, such principles as, in their opinion, shall most conduce to their own happiness, is the basis, on which the whole American fabric has been erected. The exercise of this original right is a very great exertion; nor can it, nor ought it to be frequently repeated. The principles, therefore, so established, are deemed fundamental. And as the authority, from which they proceed, is supreme, and can seldom act, they are designed to be permanent.

This original and supreme will organizes the government, and assigns, to different departments, their respective powers.

commences with assumptions about the proper and legitimate sources of law. The root premises of the law are legal text, the intent of the people who wrote the text, judicial precedent, and our people's traditions. Legal rules as well as policies arise from these ultimate sources of law, and they form the basis for all legitimate legal arguments.

CHAPTER 24

Discovering a Court's Judicial Philosophy and Your Own Philosophy of Life

The central purpose of this book was to help you learn to identify, create, attack, and evaluate the five types of legal argument to improve your skill as a legal professional. However, the types of legal argument are relevant not only to law students, lawyers, and judges, but to all persons. Everyone has a preferred mode of analysis, a philosophy of life. Here is what Justice Cardozo had to say on the subject:

> We are reminded by William James in a telling page of his lectures on Pragmatism that every one of us has in truth an underlying philosophy of life, even those of us to whom the names and notions of philosophy are unknown or anathema. There is in each of us a stream of tendency, whether you choose to call it philosophy or not, which gives coherence and direction to thought and action. Judges cannot escape that current any more than other mortals. All their lives, forces which they do not recognize and cannot name, have been tugging at them — inherited instincts, traditional beliefs, acquired convictions; and the resultant is an outlook on life, a conception of social needs, a sense in James' phrase of "the total push and pressure of the cosmos," which,

> when reasons are nicely balanced, must determine where
> choice shall fall.[461]

A judge's "outlook on life" helps to mold his or her "judicial philosophy," that is, "the belief that certain forms of argument may provide a legitimate basis for a judicial decision."[462] The jurisprudential styles of justices on the Supreme Court of the United States have been carefully scrutinized to detect these patterns of preference for particular types of legal argument. On the present Supreme Court, Justice Scalia is drawn to text and tradition.[463] Justice Kennedy and Justice Souter tend to adhere to precedent.[464] For Justice Steven Breyer, arguments based on legislative intent and policy analysis take precedence.[465]

---

461. CARDOZO, THE NATURE OF THE JUDICIAL PROCESS, *supra* note 1, at 12.

462. "What, after all, is 'judicial philosophy,' if it is not the belief that certain forms of argument may provide a legitimate basis for a judicial decision?" Bobbitt, *Reflections*, *supra* note 22, at 1920. Bobbitt notes, however, that "it is usually more a matter of emphasis and style (style for a judge being the preference for certain forms of argument over others) than complete rejection." *Id.*

463. Justice Scalia's devotion to "plain meaning" is discussed in Chapter 3. In particular, Justice Scalia practices a "philological" brand of textualism. "For Scalia, the ordinary social and dictionary meaning of individual words is the most important, and often decisive, ingredient of his analysis of a constitutional provision." David M. Zlotnik, *Justice Scalia and His Critics: An Exploration of Scalia's Fidelity to His Constitutional Methodology*, 48 EMORY L.J. 1377, 1389 (1999).

464. One scholar has stated that a hallmark of the moderate brand of jurisprudence practiced by Justices Kennedy, Souter, and former Justice Sandra Day O'Conner is "respect for precedent." Ernest Young, *Rediscovering Conservatism: Burkean Political Theory and Constitutional Interpretation*, 72 N.C. L. REV. 619, 717 (1994). Justices Scalia and Black, on the other hand, resist precedent: "[N]o two justices in this century have called for overruling more precedents than Justices Black and Scalia." Michael J. Gerhardt, *A Tale of Two Textualists: A Critical Comparison of Justices Black and Scalia*, 74 B.U. L. REV. 25, 33 (1994).

465. When Breyer was nominated to the Supreme Court, one scholar predicted that "[t]he opinions he authors or influences will include significant discussions of legislative intent, the factual context in which the

Among former members of the Supreme Court, Justice Hugo Black was a textualist,[466] Felix Frankfurter often cited tradition,[467] while Justice William Brennan and Justice Thurgood Marshall relied principally upon policy analysis.[468] Had he ascended to the Supreme Court, Judge Robert Bork would in all likelihood have remained an originalist.[469]

---

dispute arises, and the likely consequences of alternative resolutions of the dispute." Richard J. Pierce, Jr., *Justice Breyer: Intentionalist, Pragmatist, and Empiricist*, 8 ADMIN. L.J. AM. U. 747, 751 (1995). This prediction was borne out by Justice Breyer's opinion in the *Denver Area* case, discussed in Chapter 20.

466. Like Justice Scalia, Justice Black was drawn to bright line rules and textual analysis; unlike Scalia, Black rejected tradition as an interpretive modality. Gerhardt, *supra* note 464, at 26–27, 51–52. (1994).

467. Justice Frankfurter cited "[d]eeply embedded traditional ways of conducting government" to define the power of the President in Youngstown Sheet & Tube. *See* text accompanying note 116 *supra*.

468. *See* Ruggero J. Aldisert, *The Brennan Legacy: The Art of Judging*, 32 LOY. L.A. L. REV. 673 (1999) (identifying Brennan with the realist jurisprudential philosophy of Oliver Wendell Holmes, Roscoe Pound, and Benjamin Cardozo). Justice Marshall expressed his jurisprudential philosophy in his dissenting opinion in *United States v. Kras*, 409 U.S. 434 (1973), wherein he presented the following consequentialist analysis:

It may be easy for some people to think that weekly savings of less than $2 are no burden. But no one who has had close contact with poor people can fail to understand how close to the margin of survival many of them are. A sudden illness, for example, may destroy whatever savings they may have accumulated, and by eliminating a sense of security may destroy the incentive to save in the future. A pack or two of cigarettes may be, for them, not a routine purchase but a luxury indulged in only rarely. The desperately poor almost never go to see a movie, which the majority seems to believe is an almost weekly activity. They have more important things to do with what little money they have—like attempting to provide some comforts for a gravely ill child, as Kras must do.

Id. at 460.

469. In THE TEMPTING OF AMERICA (1990), Robert Bork remained convinced that "original intent" is the only legitimate technique for interpreting the Constitution:

It is probable that all judges, not just members of the Supreme Court, tend to find one or more types of argument more persuasive than others. By studying prior judicial opinions and by listening carefully in open court, you can discover the preferred jurisprudential style of the judges before whom you appear, and you can tailor your briefs and oral arguments with that in mind.

The five types of argument also have application outside the field of law. The rules of morality and religion, like rules of law, are established by reference to text, intent, precedent, tradition and policy. Which type of argument appeals to you? Are you a textualist, an intentionalist, or a traditionalist? Are you bound to precedent, or are you drawn to policy analysis? Which of these methods of analysis resonates with your deepest religious and moral convictions? What attracts you to one form of argument over another? How do you tell right from wrong?

In truth, only the approach of original understanding meets the criteria that any theory of constitutional adjudication must meet in order to possess democratic legitimacy. Only that approach is consonant with the design of the American Republic.

Id. at 143.

Index to Authors and Judges

The following authors and judges are cited or quoted at the page indicated.

Index to Cases

Topical Index